# HAL LEONARD
# GUITAR METHOD

# GUITAR TECHNIQUES

BY MICHAEL MUELLER

T0081970

Speed • Pitch • Balance • Loop

To access audio, visit:
**www.halleonard.com/mylibrary**

Enter Code
1690-0325-7308-5268

ISBN 978-1-4234-4272-1

Visit Hal Leonard Online at
**www.halleonard.com**

Contact us:
**Hal Leonard**
7777 West Bluemound Road
Milwaukee, WI 53213
Email: info@halleonard.com

In Europe, contact:
**Hal Leonard Europe Limited**
42 Wigmore Street
Marylebone, London, W1U 2RN
Email: info@halleonardeurope.com

In Australia, contact:
**Hal Leonard Australia Pty. Ltd.**
4 Lentara Court
Cheltenham, Victoria, 3192 Australia
Email: info@halleonard.com.au

# INTRODUCTION

Through the years, countless books have been published for beginning guitarists with the intent of teaching scales, chords, arpeggios, theory, harmony, and almost any other topic you can shake a pick at—except one—how to properly execute the mechanical techniques required to actually *play* the guitar. What is a hammer-on? An oblique bend? Koto picking? The answers to these questions—and plenty more—are contained in these pages as one quick, easy-to-use reference guide simply titled *Guitar Techniques*.

*Guitar Techniques* should be approached as a toolbox, with all the techniques contained herein acting as your tools for building great guitar music. Scales and chords and their accompanying theory and harmony are the raw materials that you will shape into music using these tools. With *Guitar Techniques*, you will be able to wade through transcription songbooks more easily, and your own compositions will benefit as well. Now, when you play a G–C–D chord progression, you can ask yourself, "Should I fingerpick these chords using Travis picking? Should I strum the chords? Maybe I could play them as tapped arpeggios." Hopefully, you'll find your creative juices overflowing with possibilities for even the simplest of song ideas.

*Guitar Techniques* is basically divided into two main sections. The first deals with techniques performed by the fret hand, such as vibrato, bending, and legato techniques. The second half of the book covers techniques performed by your picking hand, including fingerpicking, flatpicking, and tapping. Additionally, I've included some fairly off-the-wall miscellaneous techniques in the final section of the book for the adventurous among you. Throughout, concepts are combined and built upon to help you learn how these techniques work together. The examples range from elementary to quite complex, with the complex examples typically representing combinations of the simple ones as they are often utilized in a musical context. Each musical figure in *Guitar Techniques* has a matching audio track, as it is vital to hear these various techniques performed correctly. Where appropriate, the examples are performed at both normal and slow speed.

# CONTENTS

# THE GUITAR

Before we get started, it's important to know the parts of your guitar.

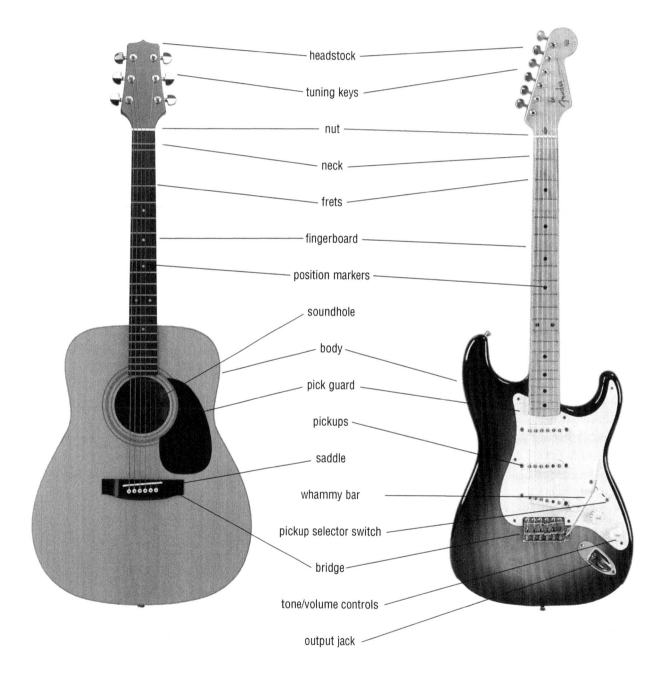

- headstock
- tuning keys
- nut
- neck
- frets
- fingerboard
- position markers
- soundhole
- body
- pick guard
- pickups
- saddle
- whammy bar
- pickup selector switch
- bridge
- tone/volume controls
- output jack

# FRET
# HAND
# TECHNIQUES

# FRETTING THE NOTES

The most fundamental fret-hand technique is simply fretting the notes. Without even touching the neck, you can play six notes—the tones produced by the six open strings on your guitar. On the neck of your guitar, there are metal wires that are perpendicular to the strings. These are called frets. By placing a finger between two of these wires and pressing down on the string, you change the length of the string that's allowed to vibrate, thus producing a different pitch than that of the open string. Depending on the model of guitar you're using, you probably have between twenty and twenty-four frets available to you. When you consider that there are also six strings, there are between 120 and 144 notes you can play on your guitar, not including special techniques—that's more than a piano!

In terms of actually fretting a note, where you place your finger is important for generating a clear tone. Ideally, you'll want to press on the string slightly forward of the midpoint between frets. This prevents you from having to use excess force to hold the string down, while at the same time, eliminates player-generated fret buzz.

# POSITION

As you read through songbooks or other printed lessons, you may encounter a phrase that reads something like this: "…plays an E minor pentatonic lick at twelfth position." Let's take a moment to explain the concept of position. In positional playing, each finger of your fret hand is assigned one fret, and the position is named for the fret at which the first finger is located when playing a scale or lick. So, in first position, your index finger plays the notes on the first fret, your middle finger plays the notes on the second fret, your ring finger plays the notes on the third fret, and your pinky finger plays the notes on the fourth fret.

Using the first-position chromatic line in Fig. 1, let's give it a whirl.

Fig. 1

TRACK 1   ♩ = 60

Be sure to try this exercise in every position on the fretboard. Because the fret widths get smaller as you move up the fretboard, you'll notice a slightly different feel in different areas of the neck. To begin your experimentation, try the same exercise in fifth position (Fig. 2). Remember to keep each of your fret-hand fingers slightly forward of the midpoint between the frets.

Fig. 2

TRACK 2  ♩ = 60

# VIBRATO

Now that you're comfortable fretting notes on the fingerboard, it's time to do something with the note to make it a bit more exciting. Perhaps the most popular way of adding subtle texture or providing dynamic enhancement to a note is through a technique called *vibrato*. Vibrato is simply a repeated fluctuation in pitch. On the guitar, vibrato is performed primarily with the fret-hand fingers or through the use of the whammy bar.

There are two main techniques for fret-hand vibrato: parallel-to-the-string movement favored by classical guitarists and the more popular perpendicular-to-the-string movement favored by rock, pop, and blues guitarists. In the classical style, the vibrato is achieved by shifting the pressure of your finger forward and backward along the length of the string (without changing fret positions). Contrary to the previous lesson on fretting notes, the classical-style vibrato works best when the note is fretted closer to the middle position between two fretwires. As you apply pressure toward the bridge, there is a slight decrease in tension on the string, thus lowering its pitch. Then, as you apply pressure toward the nut, there is a slight increase in tension on the string, resulting in an increase in pitch. This gives classical-style vibrato a very important distinction: it is the only vibrato that raises *and* lowers the pitch of the fretted note.

Fig. 3

TRACK 3  ♩ = 70

More commonly, strings are pushed or pulled perpendicular to their length to produce pitch fluctuations, or vibrato. In this manner, the note is alternately raised and returned to normal pitch, with the width of the vibrato dependent upon the physical deviation. The most common variation of this technique is a pivot vibrato. In this type of vibrato, your thumb is anchored at the top of the fretboard to provide counterforce, and by rotating your arm back and forth about its long axis, the pitch of the note is raised by slightly bending the string and then releasing it.

B.B. King is famous for his version of the *pivot* vibrato, known as the "butterfly" vibrato. The technique gets its name from the visual effect created when B.B. vibratoes notes with his index finger while fanning out the remaining fingers. The resulting sound is a tight, rapidly fluctuating vibrato that is, in Eric Clapton's words, "...the kind of vibrato you would die for." Remember, though, it's more important to sound good than to look cool, so don't worry about looking like the King when you play; focus on copping the sound of his legendary vibrato. Play the blues licks in Fig. 4, and work hard at achieving a crisp, tight vibrato where indicated.

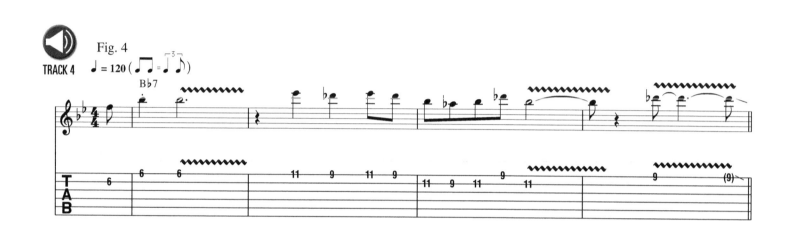

In the previous section, I mentioned Eric Clapton's praise of B.B. King; however, ol' Slowhand also deserves vibratory accolades. Rather than pivoting or rotating his arm and wrist to produce vibrato, Clapton generates his singing sound from the upper arm. If you watch him closely, you'll see that his fret hand "floats" around the fretboard unanchored. And when he produces vibrato, he rotates his arm about the elbow (tiny bicep curls!).While this sound is quite distinctive, it is also very difficult to master with precision. By using your elbow as the fulcrum, you leave a lot of room for error, so I don't recommend this technique as a starter. But as I said, it does have a very distinct sound, and if you're looking to clone Clapton's touch, this is how it's done.

The last type of vibrato I'd like to discuss is simply a stylistic variation on the perpendicular vibrato technique. An exaggerated, wide vibrato, performed slowly or rapidly, can be a very effective dramatic tool. To set some concrete parameters, I'll define a wide vibrato as no less than a quarter-step deviation from the fretted pitch.

This type of vibrato requires a little more attention than a tight pivot vibrato, as there is more room for inconsistency, and thus it's easier for the listener to hear mistakes. For example, if you're applying a half-step deviation, it is imperative that each repetition be a half-step because playing flat or sharp in this scenario is quite evident—particularly with a slow vibrato. You should be aware, however, that there exists a beneficial paradox in wide vibrato, in terms of accuracy and speed. The faster you apply a wide vibrato, the more difficult it is to consistently nail the pitch deviation. Conveniently, however, it's also more difficult for a listener to notice slight variations. On the other hand, a slower wide vibrato makes it easier to be consistent in your deviation, but it's also easier for the listener to hear mistakes. What this comes down to is that you should work carefully on achieving a consistent vibrato, regardless of which style you adapt.

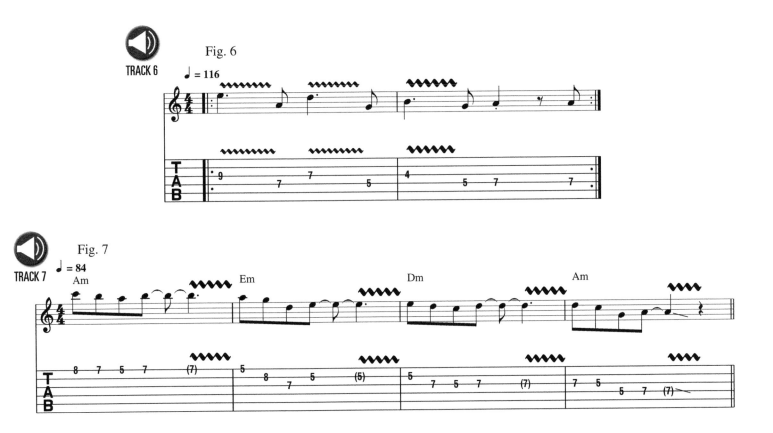

Now that you've tried and listened to all of these vibrato types, take the time to master each of them. Vibrato is one of the fundamental expressionistic techniques you can use on the guitar to help create your own voice.

As you work with these vibrato techniques, don't box yourself into worrying about common associations. In other words, feel free to try using the classical vibratro technique in a rock or blues setting. Try employing an extra-wide vibrato in a jazz guitar solo. The possibilities are limited only by your imagination.

# BENDING

After vibrato, probably the most popular expressive technique used in playing the guitar is string bending. Bending a string after striking a note raises the pitch in proportion to the increased tension on the string. A bend can be defined by either the number of steps it represents in a scale or in terms of musical intervals. The purpose of string bending is to give your melody lines a more "singing-like" quality—it allows you to access the "in-between" notes that aren't represented on the standard fretboard. An experienced, wily string bender can make his or her guitar roar with the fire of Jimi Hendrix or cry like a country pedal steel guitar.

Of course, to achieve these metaphors, you'll need to have a thorough understanding and command of a variety of bending techniques at your fingertips. These include single-string bends, double-stop bends, ghost bends, unison bends, and oblique bends. And with all of these various techniques, there is still the parameter of how wide of an interval to to play. So, I'll also discuss a range of deviation from quarter-step to 2½-step bends and where they're most effective.

There is also the question of what to do with the note once it's bent to the proper pitch. Do you simply let it ring? Sometimes. Hey, what if you apply a vibrato technique on top of the bend? That's a common measure taken in great guitar music. What if I just want to bend the note up to its target pitch and then stop it? You can do that too; it's a technique called choking. Finally, you can simply release the bend back to sound the fretted note. It's up to you and your creative direction.

## SINGLE-STRING BENDS

The most elementary bend is the single-string bend. These can be performed on any of your six strings, however, they are most commonly applied on strings 1, 2, and 3. Half- and whole-step bends are the most popular single-string bends and are commonly found in rock, country, blues, and metal. Before I let you loose on a musical example, let's go over a few performance tips. First, the most common finger with which you'll bend strings is your ring finger. When you bend a string with this finger, you don't need to do it in isolation. In other words, use your index and middle fingers to assist the ring finger [see photo]. The same goes for bends with the middle or pinky fingers too. Use whatever fingers are available to help you crank out the bend, especially if you use heavy-gauge strings. (Stevie Ray Vaughan used .013s!)

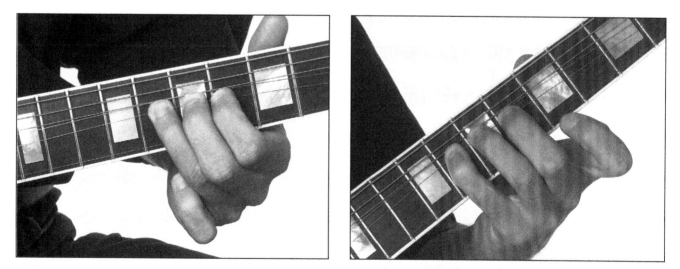

To ensure proper intonation of the bend, first play the target note on the fretboard, and then bend up to that note and match its pitch. So, if you're required to bend a D note on the third string at the seventh fret up to pitch E, first play the E as a fretted note (third string, ninth fret). Then strike the D note and bend the string until its pitch matches the E note that you just played. Use this exercise for all of your bends until your ear has a firm grasp of what a half- or whole-step bend sounds like. The example in Fig. 8 contains several bending opportunities. Use the pitch-matching exercise prior to each bend until you can nail the pitches without it.

Fig. 8

TRACK 8

The quarter-step bend is another type of single-string bend. It is found in several musical genres but is truly at home in the blues. In fact, the note that's attained by performing a quarter-step bend is often called a "blue note," because of its status as an "in-between" note. Due to the physical layout of the pentatonic minor and blues scales on the fretboard (the two most commonly used scales in blues), quarter-step bends are often performed with the index finger.

Getting the correct intonation for these bends is a little trickier than half- or whole-step bends, as you can't fret the target note for reference. What you can do, however, is play the note one half step above the original note, bend up to that note, and try to mentally mark the halfway point between the two pitches, which is the quarter-step pitch. Don't worry, your ear will in all likelihood adapt to this interval quite quickly, and you'll have no problem tearing these off at will. Try the phrase below for some common uses of quarter-note bends.

Fig. 9

TRACK 9

The final set of single-note bends includes bends greater than one whole step. String manufacturers love these bends, as you're more likely to break strings while performing them. When done properly, they give the illusion that you're using a whammy bar. Try the bends below, and remember to find your target note first to practice achieving correct intonation. (A 1½-step bend is equivalent to three frets; a two-step bend is equivalent to four frets; a 2½-step bend is equivalent to five (!) frets.) And don't forget to use your other fingers to help achieve these monster bends.

Fig. 10

TRACK 10

# GHOST BENDS

A simple variation that adds a lot of character to your bends is the *ghost bend*, or *pre-bend*. This type of bend requires you to bend the note prior to striking a note, so you're bending blindly (or should I say "deafly"?).

Ghost bends most commonly come in the form of half- or whole-step prebends (rarely anything different), and can be practiced in the same manner as normal single-string bends by first playing the target note, and then trying to match it. For this technique, however, you'll be relying on "feel" in your fingers. With time and practice, you'll know just how far to bend the string before striking it to produce the note.

The same rules also apply to ghost bends and to normal single-string bends when it comes to what you can do with it once it's sounded. Add vibrato, choke it, release it—it's entirely up to you. The phrase in Fig. 11 contains one of the most popular uses for ghost bends—emulating a pedal steel guitar.

Fig. 11

TRACK 11 ♩ = 144

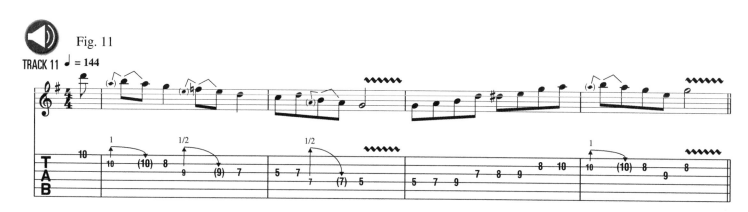

# UNISON BENDS

Now that you've got single-string bending down pat, let's toss in another variation that not only sounds cool but will help you achieve good intonation in your bends as well. This new type of bend is called a *unison* bend. A unison bend requires you to bend a note up to a pitch matching a fretted note on an adjacent string that remains stationary and is sounded either sequentially or simultaneously. These bends usually occur on either strings 1 and 2 or strings 2 and 3. Fig. 12 contains unison bends on strings 2 and 3. Use your index finger to fret string 2, and bend string 3 with your ring finger.

Fig. 12

TRACK 12 ♩ = 120

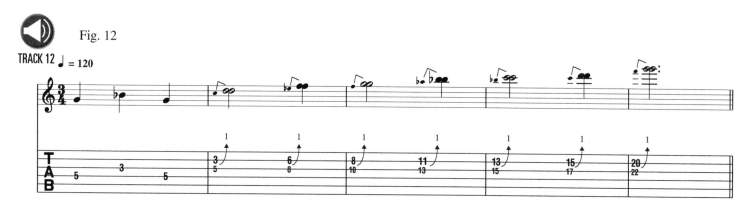

Notice that some of the unison bends in the following figure occur on strings 1 and 2. Because the notes are situated three frets apart, you'll need to bend with either your pinky finger or stretch your ring finger an extra fret and perform the bend. Whichever way you choose to do it, use your other fingers to help you perform the bend.

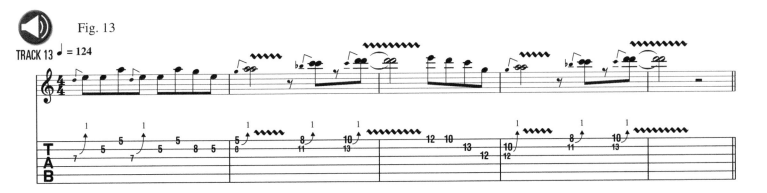

Fig. 13

TRACK 13 ♩ = 124

## OBLIQUE BENDS

There's another technique that involves two strings, one bent while the other remains stationary; however, the two pitches that are produced do not match. This is called an *oblique bend*. You may have noticed that in the unison bends, your fret-hand index finger played the stationary note. In oblique bends, generally the pinky (and sometimes the middle or ring) fingers are responsible for the stationary note. These bends are quite popular in rock, country, and rockabilly music, and often incorporate more than one stationary note.

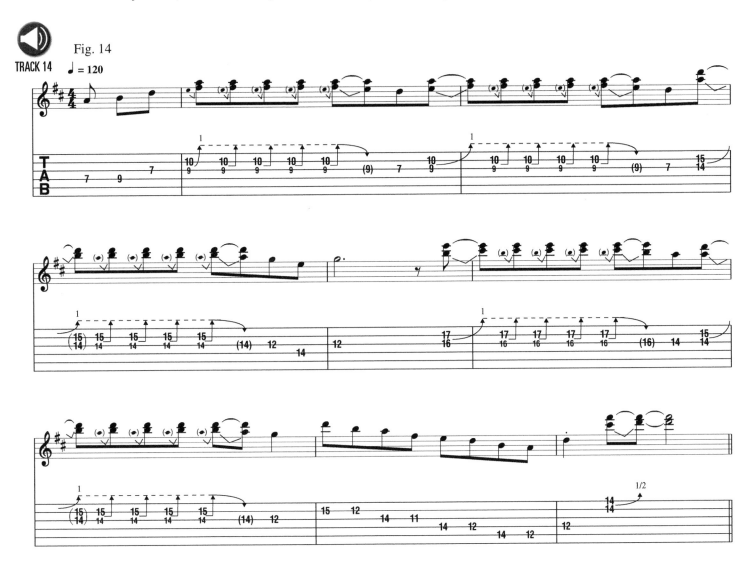

Fig. 14

TRACK 14 ♩ = 120

# DOUBLE-STOP BENDS

Sometimes, you just need a downright mean and nasty sounding lick, and one of the coolest techniques for producing that kind of attitude is the double-stop bend. A "double stop" is simply two strings played at once—a two-note chord, or, a dyad, if you will. Blues, funk, rock, and particularly country players have done amazing things with double stops over the years, one of which is bending them.

There are two ways to perform *double-stop bends*. You can either assign one fret-hand finger to each of the notes to be attacked, or as is more commonly done, simply barre one fret-hand finger over both notes. When bending a double stop with the barre technique, pull the strings away from you (toward the floor). This will help prevent string slippage due to the shape of your finger pad.

The performance technique you use partially depends on the magnitude of pitch deviation desired. If, for example, you're bending one string a full step and the other a half-step, you may wish to use separate fingers for each string simply for strength reasons. On the other hand, if you're bending one string a half step and the other a quarter step, a simple barre should do the trick. Now, you may be asking yourself, how can I bend two different strings two different amounts with only one finger? It happens quite naturally, actually. Say, for example, you're bending strings 2 and 3 using the barre approach with your ring finger. Start by bending both strings a quarter step. Then, gradually place more pressure on the finger tip while pulling down. This will enable you to continue bending the third string to a half step while second remains bent only a quarter step.

The important thing to remember when playing double-stop bends is to play them with attitude and authority. Try the examples below, and, at first, find your target pitches prior to attempting the bends, in the same manner you did before. But eventually, you'll want to pull these off based on the physical feel combined with your ear. Remember: Attitude!

Fig. 15

# MUTING

An integral part of playing cleanly is a technique called *muting*. You can mute strings with either your fret hand or picking hand, but for now, we'll concentrate on fret-hand muting.

The most basic form of fret-hand muting is simply laying your fret-hand fingers across the strings with gentle pressure, but not enough to actually fret or sound notes. If you've ever listened to funk guitar, you've undoubtedly heard this type of muting. It's also very popular in blues and reggae forms. The example below contains no actual sounding notes. It's just a rhythmical figure to help get you used to the feel of the muting technique. If you hear harmonics (see next section), try muting the strings at a different position on the neck.

Fig. 16

Now, let's mix in a few chords between the muted strums. To most efficiently play this style, keep the chord fingerings in place while you play the muted strums, but lift your fingers off the strings just enough to prevent the notes from sounding. When it comes time to actually sound a chord, simply press down a little harder.

Fig. 17

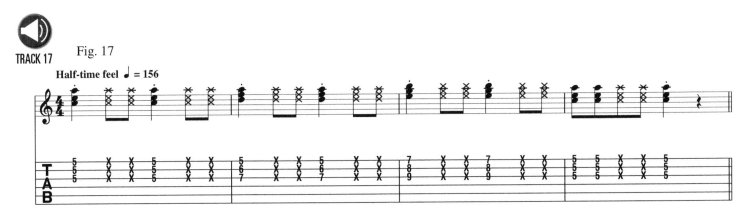

Another important technique that falls into the muting category is *finger rolling*. Though the name is a bit strange, the technique is essential. Finger rolling is useful when playing sequential notes at the same fret but on different strings. Say, for example, you were going to play the A note at the fifth fret of the sixth string followed by the D note at the fifth fret of the fifth string. Rather than lifting your index finger off the sixth string and moving it to the fifth string, you can simply play the sixth-string note with the tip of your index finger, and then flatten, or roll, your finger downward to play the fifth-string note, muting the sixth string in the process. Try playing a descending and ascending A minor pentatonic scale arranged in 4ths. Be sure not to allow two notes at the same fret position to ring together!

Here's a classic blues lick that combines the finger rolling technique with a couple of others you've learned thus far.

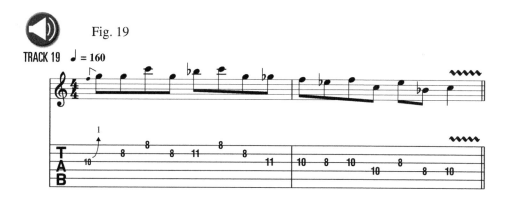

# NATURAL HARMONICS

In some songs, you may have noticed cool-sounding, bell-like tones coming from the guitar. These are called *natural harmonics*, and are produced by lightly touching the string over certain node points. Conveniently—but by no means coincidental—the most common and easily produced harmonics happen to have their node points directly above the metal fretwire in a few key locations on the fretboard. Here's how it happens.

Without going into too much dry, physics detail, harmonics are a naturally occurring phenomenon of string vibration. When a string is plucked and allowed to ring openly, the tone produced is called the fundamental. By lightly touching the string at the midpoint of its length (twelfth fret) prior to striking it, we cause the string to vibrate in halves, thus producing the first harmonic, a pitch exactly one octave above the fundamental. By lightly touching the string at one-third of its length (seventh fret), we produce the second harmonic, an octave plus a perfect fifth above the fundamental. Touch it at one quarter of its length (fifth fret), and you produce the third harmonic, exactly two octaves above the fundamental.

For a summary of the common open harmonics and their location on the fretboard, refer to the figure below.

# OPEN HARMONICS

| Fundamental (open string) | E | A | D | G | B | E |
|---|---|---|---|---|---|---|
| 1st Harmonic (12th fret) | E | A 8va | D 8va | G 8va | B 8va | E 8va |
| 2nd Harmonic (7th/19th fret) | B | E 8va + P5 | A 8va + P5 | D 8va + P5 | F♯ 8va + P5 | B 8va + P5 |
| 3rd Harmonic (5th/24th fret) | E | A 15ma | D 15ma | G 15ma | B 15ma | E 15ma |

OK, the physics lesson is over. Let's try playing some of these harmonics! If your guitar doesn't have twenty-four frets, play those harmonics at the theoretical twenty-fourth fret, which is approximately over the neck pick-up on a Strat or Les Paul-style guitar.

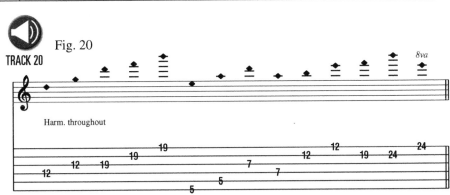

Fig. 20

Were you able to produce all of those harmonics? Good. Though they sound cool on their own, it's much more exciting (and ear-catching) to incorporate them into your melodies. If you feel comfortable playing harmonics by themselves, you're ready to try tossing them in among normally fretted notes or to try quickly changing positions.

Fig. 21

TRACK 21

♩ = 124

Feel free to explore other harmonic locations as well. Try tremolo picking (rapid alternation of downstrokes and upstrokes on a single string) on the open A string. As you begin, lightly touch the string over the first fret, and begin to slowly move your fret hand toward the bridge, maintaining a light touch on the string. Use plenty of distortion to help bring out the stubborn ones and note the locations that produce strong harmonics (besides those already listed in the chart) for future use.

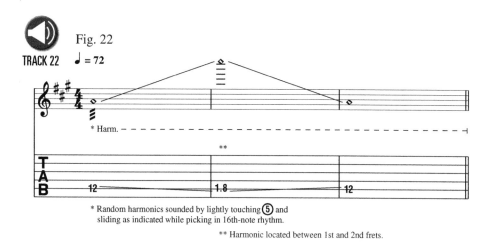

Fig. 22

TRACK 22    ♩ = 72

\* Random harmonics sounded by lightly touching ⑤ and
sliding as indicated while picking in 16th-note rhythm.

\*\* Harmonic located between 1st and 2nd frets.

## PALM HARMONICS

This manner of moving harmonics up and down the neck is a technique in itself. In fact, it can also be done while keeping your fret hand stationary, and slowly moving your pick hand up and down the neck—a technique known as *palm harmonics*. With your fret hand, trill (see next chapter) between two notes, and while lightly touching the same string with the edge of your pick-hand palm, move your pick hand from the bridge toward the nut (and back again).

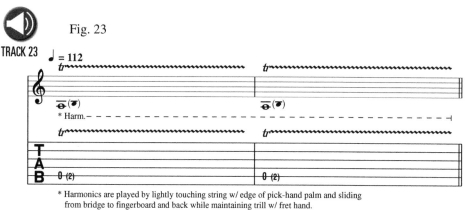

Fig. 23

TRACK 23    ♩ = 112

\* Harmonics are played by lightly touching string w/ edge of pick-hand palm and sliding
from bridge to fingerboard and back while maintaining trill w/ fret hand.

## LEGATO

So far, you've had to pick every note you've played in *Guitar Techniques*. But there's a way to produce notes on the guitar without a pick attack: *legato* technique. Legato is an Italian term that is most simply translated as "smooth." Hence, the adjectives that are often used to describe legato lines are words such as "smooth," "fluid," or "liquid." Well-executed legato lines just seem to flow unimpeded from the fingers and soul, so it's a technique worth getting under your fingers.

Legato playing is made up of three basic techniques: hammer-ons, pull-offs, and slides. A fourth, the trill, is actually the combination of hammer-ons and pull-offs and will also be covered in this unit. These techniques are heard largely in rock, blues, and fusion contexts, but are also found in country and jazz as well.

## Hammer-Ons

The first legato technique is called a *hammer-on*. The hammer-on gets its name from the action taken by your fingers to produce the note: you actually "hammer" one of your fret-hand fingers onto the string causing a note to ring out. Play the open-position E minor pentatonic scale below to get a feel for the technique. Be sure to pick the open string before you hammer onto the fretted note.

You don't have to begin with an open string to perform hammer-ons. You can fret any note and proceed to hammer on a note further up the fretboard. You can even use your picking hand to do this, but we'll cover that later in the book. The C minor pentatonic scale below offers the chance to perform hammer-ons from a fretted note. As with the open strings in the previous example, you'll need to pick the notes at the eighth fret and then hammer onto the subsequent note.

It's also important to be able to perform hammer-ons with any combination of fret-hand fingers. You don't always get to start with the index finger. The following exercise will help you build consistency and strength using all combinations of fret-hand fingers. Be sure that all of the notes—both picked and hammered-on—ring out at the same volume.

Now that you're feeling cozy with that, let's put a rock-star lick in your growing bag of tricks. To sound really cool, string together a couple of hammer-ons on the same string. Try playing the C major scale pattern below. It's arranged for you to play three notes per string, which, when performed at a fast tempo, is quite impressive-sounding!

Fig. 27

TRACK 27

## Pull-Offs

Hopefully, you're thinking, "If I can play a note, and then hammer on to a higher note, can I also play a note, and then pull off to a lower note?" The answer is "Yes!" Eternal cousin to the mighty hammer-on is the equally mighty *pull-off*. Performed just the way it sounds, you simply strike a fretted note, and then pull your finger off that note to sound either a lower fretted note or an open string. Note that you do not simply *lift* your finger off the string. You need to pull the string—slightly—toward the floor, and let your finger come off naturally. Be careful not to change the pitch of the note, however. Here are the two minor pentatonic scales you played with hammer-ons before, only this time, they're descending scales with pull-offs.

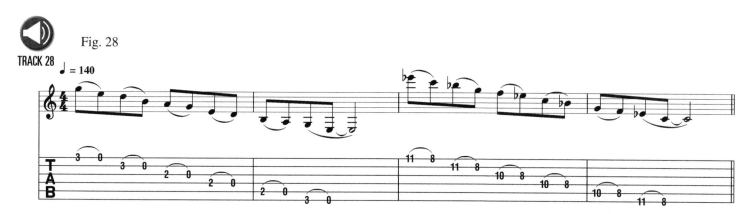

Fig. 28

TRACK 28

And just like hammer-ons, you can string together pull-offs. Here's that C major scale again—ascending with hammer-ons and descending with pull-offs.

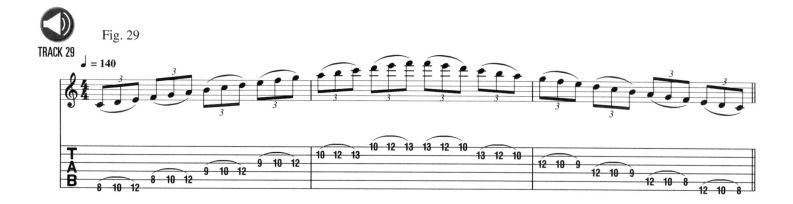

Fig. 29

TRACK 29

Now, let's combine some hammer-ons and pull-offs. You can start either on an open string or a fretted note. Strike the note, hammer on to a higher note, and without restriking the string, pull off to the original pitch. The example below contains several of these combinations.

Fig. 30

Also, as with the hammer-ons and pull-offs independently, you can string together several successive hammer-ons and pull-offs. Let's try that C major scale one more time. This one—when played at a swift tempo—will really make some heads turn. But take it slowly, making sure that each note rings at equal volume. Notice that you're playing seven notes per string, but you only pick each string once—on the initial attack.

Fig. 31

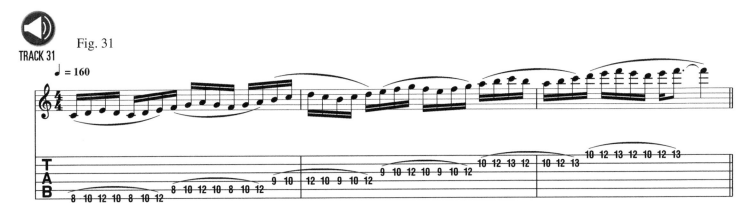

### Trills

Going back to basics a bit from the previous example, let's just try hammering on and pulling off between two notes. But this time, hammer on and pull off as rapidly as you can. This rapid alternation between two notes is called a *trill*. This technique is commonly employed in classical music, but has also found a special place in the improvisational hearts of blues guitarists over the years.

Fig. 32

## Slides

Think back to when we talked about bending strings. You began with a fretted note and then bent the string so the fretted note would match the pitch of a note one, two, or three frets further up the neck. Now, it's time to show you another way of reaching that note: sliding up to it. Slides are performed in two ways: You can strike the initial note and then slide your finger along the length of the string (up or down) to the target pitch without restriking the string. This is called a "slurred slide." Alternatively, you might want to perform the same slide, but strike the target note. In this case, the slide is referred to as a "shift slide."

Fig. 33

TRACK 33  ♩ = 160

These sliding techniques are incredibly effective tools for moving around the fretboard. Whereas with bends the range of deviation is limited by string tension and risk of string breakage, sliding a note eliminates that risk. Also, if you use heavy-gauge strings, you'll find sliding notes to be much more comfortable. You'll find that jazzers use slides a lot, for both aurally aesthetic reasons (they sound cool) and practical reasons (jazzers tend to use heavy strings). Additionally, you can slide octaves—a staple of jazz guitar—much easier than you can bend them. Give this one a whirl.

Fig. 34

TRACK 34  ♩ = 144

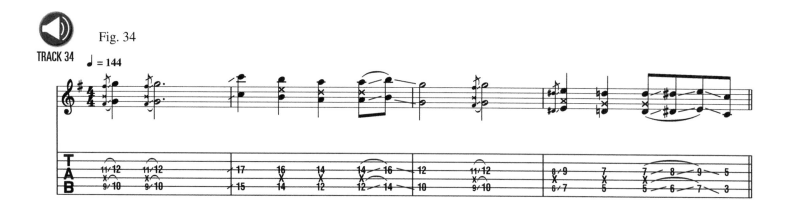

# SLIDE GUITAR

Not to be confused with the term introduced in the previous section, *slide guitar* requires an extra piece of equipment: the slide. Slides come in several varieties, including glass, porcelain, ceramic, metal (steel or brass), and plastic. Over the years, slide guitarists have gained a reputation for being able to turn any ordinary object into a functional slide, including pill bottles, combs, ham bones, cigarette lighters, beer bottles, drumsticks, pool cues, bar glasses, mic stands, and I'm sure dozens of other odd items. In fact, you've probably heard the term "bottleneck slide." This gets its name from players who would cut off the necks of old beer or soda bottles and use the tube-like neck to make their guitars gliss with joy.

Slide guitar has been particularly abundant in blues and classic rock music. Early Delta blues guitarists played slide on their acoustic guitars, often with the strings set quite high. Later, the slide could be heard in conjunction with metal resonator guitars such as those from National and Dobro. Lap-style guitars made the rounds, eventually evolving into the pedal steel guitar that is so essential to the country sound. Finally, in the late '60s and early '70s, bands like Derek & the Dominos, Allman Brothers, and Lynyrd Skynyrd would introduce rock audiences to both the fiery and the wistful sounds of the slide.

To play slide guitar, you'll first need to choose a slide. They're available at your local guitar store, and probably in each of the varieties I described earlier. Glass seems to be the favored material for a warmer, fuller sound. Of course, glass has its downside, too. Drop it once, and it's gone! The same applies for porcelain and ceramic slides. So, if you're the clumsy type, you might want to try a metal slide. Metal produces a brigher tone than glass, with chrome being brightest but brass being warmer.

Now that you've picked a slide, let's pick some notes with it. You should wear the slide over your ring or pinky finger, whichever is more comfortable for you, and the slide should fit over at least two-thirds of whichever finger you choose.

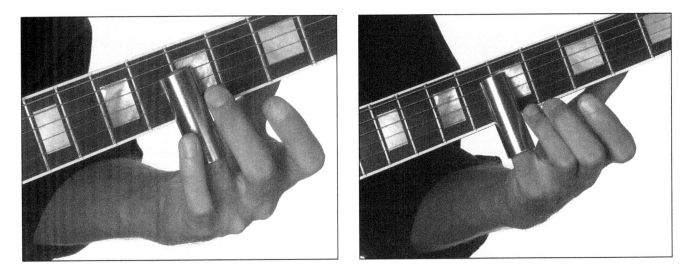

Good intonation is the key to slide guitar. Intonation means accuracy of pitch. When you play with a slide, it should be positioned directly over the fretwire, not in-between as when fretting notes. Hold the slide straight, parallel to the fretwire. Also, don't press the strings down against the fretboard. The slide should rest against the strings with enough pressure that the strings don't buzz when played, but not so much that the strings are muted.

In the example below, begin with your slide positioned at the seventh fret. Lightly touch the strings behind the slide with the index finger of your fret hand. Pluck or strum the D chord and slide up to the ninth fret to sound the E chord. Then, to play the D chord again, lift the slide off the strings and shift back to just in front of the seventh fret. Place the slide on the strings, pluck or strum, and then slide down to the seventh fret.

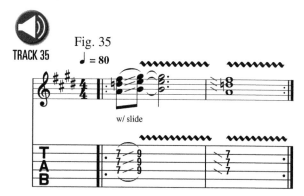

Notice the vibrato indicators in the example above. To produce vibrato with a slide, you should anchor your thumb on the back of the neck and rapidly wobble the slide back and forth from slightly behind the desired fretwire (flat) to slightly ahead of it (sharp). This technique adds sustain to the note and gives it a more "human voice" quality.

The following is an 8-bar jam in the key of G using slide guitar. Dial in a slight overdrive, adopt a husky voice, and sing the blues with this one. Have fun!

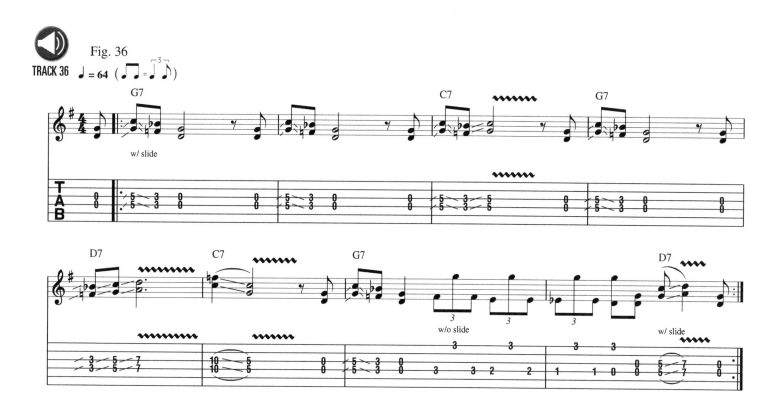

# PICK
# HAND
# TECHNIQUES

# STRUMMING

*Strumming* is one of the most elemental techniques on the guitar, and is by far the most common accompanimental technique. Strumming is basically defined as playing two or more notes with a single, unidirectional attack on the strings with either your fingers or a pick. It can be as simple as whole-, half-, or quarter-note downstrums or as complex as skanky sixteenth-note funk guitar rhythms.

A basic rule of thumb for strumming patterns is that you play the downbeats with a downstroke, and the upbeats with an upstroke:

**EIGHTH-NOTE STRUM PATTERN**

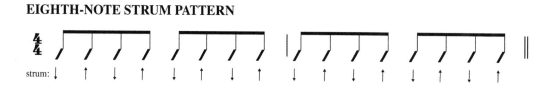

For rhythms containing sixteenth notes, just "double up" on the rule. Use downstrokes for the downbeats and the upbeats (first and third sixteenth notes of the beat, respectively), and upstrokes for the weaker sections of the beat (second and fourth sixteenth notes of the beat). If you encounter tied chords, keep your alternating motion going even though you aren't striking the tied chord. This will help you stay in the groove.

**SIXTEENTH-NOTE STRUM PATTERN**

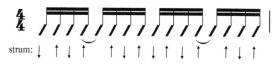

Try strumming through the following example using these basic rules. Strumming directions are provided to guide you through the piece. Strum the full chords, and try strumming from the elbow. That is, use your elbow as the pivot for your alternating strokes. If you don't have to play on a certain part of the beat, perform the physical movement as if you did, but don't strike the strings. Again, this will help keep you in the groove.

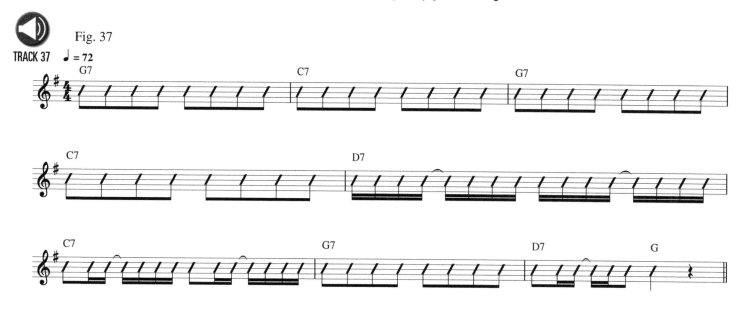

26

## Carter Strumming

Another popular form of strumming, particularly in country music, is called *Carter strumming*. Named for guitarist Maybelle Carter, this strum requires chords with the root note in the bass, and divides the chord into bass notes and treble notes, thus allowing you to play a bass line with the chords. To perform the basic Carter strum, first pick the bass note root (quarter note), then downstrum and upstrum the treble strings (eighth note each). Next, pick another bass note (preferably the 5th, but the root is acceptable), and repeat the down/up strum pattern. A common variation of the Carter strum is to alternate bass notes in an eighth note pattern. Try the following example—I think you'll catch on fast.

Here's a full 12-bar country jam, including walking bass lines at each chord change. For this strum, your wrist should serve as the pivot point instead of your elbow. Feel free to try upstrums for the chord partials, but traditionally, most players have used all downstrums in this style of accompaniment. Work through the piece slowly at first, and when you've got it down, grab your cowboy hat and spurs and kick it into a full gallop.

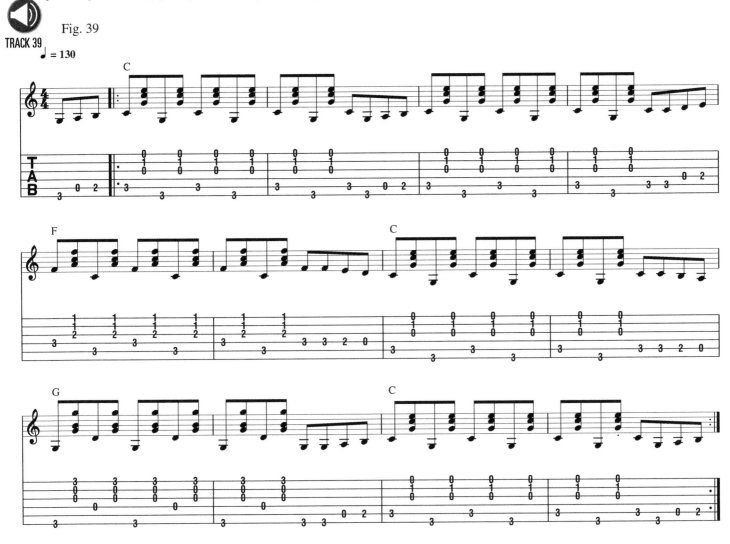

# PALM MUTING

Earlier in *Guitar Techniques*, we discussed muting techniques for the fret hand. Now, it's time to discuss how to mute with the pick hand. *Palm muting* is achieved by gently resting the pinky-side of your palm against the strings (usually near the bridge) as you play. Typically, it is used in conjunction with power chords, but palm muting can also be employed on arpeggios and single-note riffs as well. In this case, you're not muting the string entirely; you just don't allow the notes to ring out. This gives your power chords a "chunky" sound (which is usually a *good* thing when playing power chords). The following example is a common power-chord progression in a rock style. Palm-mute the chords throughout.

Fig. 40

TRACK 40 ♩ = 120

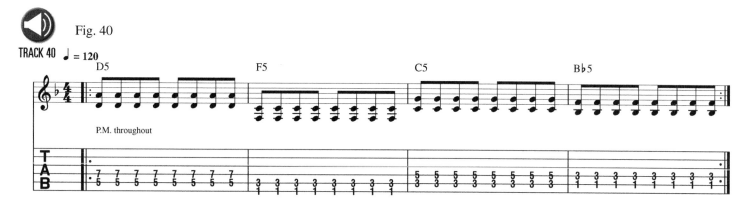

Palm muting is also commonly used with bass pedal tones. A pedal tone is a note around which other notes or chords move. Used in combination with palm muting, the pedal tone is usually muted, and the chords surrounding it are allowed to ring. This is very popular in hard rock and heavy metal music. Try your hand at the metal mania below. Keep your palm against the strings as you strike the muted bass notes, and quickly lift up when you strike the power chords.

Fig. 41

TRACK 41 ♩ = 116

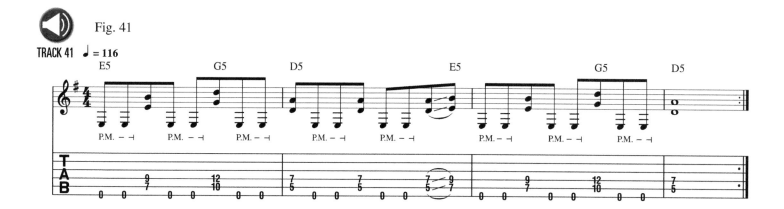

As you can see, palm muting is a very simple yet effective tool. Its role, however, extends beyond the rock applications shown here. Try using it in your single-note lines for a change of pace. Muting your lines will introduce a whole new dynamic to your playing. It's also quite effective when used in conjunction with arpeggiated chords. Don't be afraid to experiment.

# FINGERPICKING

While you can perform strumming techniques with either your fingers or a flatpick, it is commonly assumed that players use a pick for strumming. However, that typically leaves three digits on your pick hand with nothing to do. What a waste! If you're accustomed to using a flatpick, this is as good a time as any to put those wasted digits to work and try *fingerpicking*. Traditional fingerpicking technique dictates that you use your thumb (p), index (i), middle (m), and ring (a) fingers on your pick hand to attack the strings. As you can imagine, this technique opens a world of opportunity for variety in how you play chords, arpeggios, and even melodies. In the following section, we'll discuss a few of the more common fingerstyle techniques employed in popular music—just enough to pique your interest.

### Travis Picking

Taking its name from country music star Merle Travis, *Travis picking* has transcended country music and been utilized to great effect in the rock, pop, and folk styles as well. The underlying basis of Travis picking is that the thumb plays a steady bass line while the remaining three fingers (or four!) play melody notes. To position your hand correctly, rest your thumb on the top of the low E string. Then, position your index, middle, and ring fingers lightly on the underside of strings 3, 2, and 1, respectively. This prepares you to pluck downward with your thumb, and upward with your fingers. Let's try a simple example.

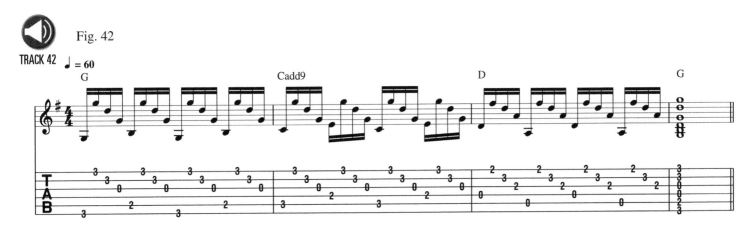

If you feel pretty comfortable using that combination of fingers, good! You have basic Travis picking under your fingers. Now, let's try to stretch the boundaries a bit and introduce the pinky into the mix. For this variation, play the sixth string with your thumb, the fourth string with your index finger, the third string with your middle finger, and the second string with your ring finger. You'll now use your pinky finger to play the notes on the first string. Also for this example, tune your low E string down one whole step to D. This is called Drop D tuning (low to high: D–A–D–G–B–E) and is very common in fingerstyle guitar.

## Fingerstyle Chords

When playing fingerstyle, you may come across chords that are not arpeggiated and should not be strummed. In cases like these, you need to pluck the chords with a combination of fingers. Similar to Travis picking, your thumb plucks the lowest note in the chord, and your index, middle, ring, and pinky fingers, play the remaining chord tones. Pluck the chords in the example below. To make things easier, each chord is arranged to contain four notes, one for each digit (except the pinky finger).

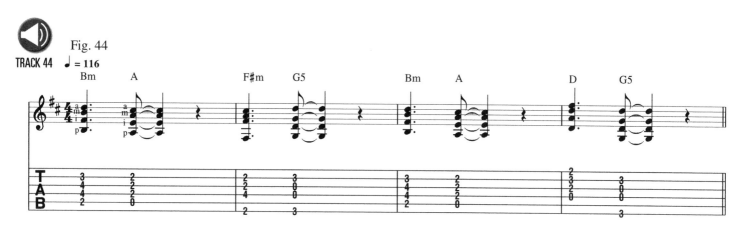

You'll hear this technique in almost all forms of music, but its heart is in jazz guitar. As jazz guitar evolved into a solo instrument, players developed chord voicings with bass notes on nonadjacent strings (broken voicings), thus separating the bass line from the chords just enought to create a credible illusion of a separate bass player in self-accompaniment. To further drive home the illusion, notes were added between chord changes to create walking bass lines. Take a swing at the jazz ballad progression below.

# FLATPICKING

I'll wager that most of the people who are using this book went through the entire first half—up to the fingerstyle chapters—using a flatpick. Typically made of plastic and coming in all sorts of shapes, sizes, and thicknesses, the flatpick has become symbolic of the guitar itself. It's the tool behind some of the finest strummin', pickin', and shreddin' ever put to record. And there are almost as many variations for using it as there are of the device itself. I'm going to take you through a few of the most common and essential techniques.

### Alternate Picking

The fundamental flatpick technique is termed *alternate picking*, which is a simple down/up/down/up (or, up/down/up/down) type of attack pattern. If there's any one flatpick technique that you must be able to produce, it's alternate picking. More than any other variation of flatpicking, alternate picking is the most intuitive in terms of rhythm and coordination. In a sense, you've already experimented with alternate picking when you worked through the strumming patterns, which required a down/up movement, found earlier in this book. Here, however, we're reducing it down to single-note lines.

For a real basic exercise to get you started, refer back to Figs. 1 and 2 in this book and play them again. This time, begin with a downstroke on the F note on the sixth string, use an upstroke for the F♯, a downstroke for the G, and an upstroke for the G♯. Do the same on the remaining strings—without missing a beat. The hardest part of alternate picking is moving from one string to another, especially if the pick stroke is counterdirectional to the physical movement toward the string. For example, if you're moving from the sixth string to the fifth string, you're moving your pick position *toward* the floor. If an upstroke is "scheduled" for the first note on the fifth string, it may at first seem a bit counterintuitive, but you'll just have to trust me: it's right. The three-note-per-string scalar example below will force you to play this way on several strings. Take your time and play it cleanly. Speed will come with practice.

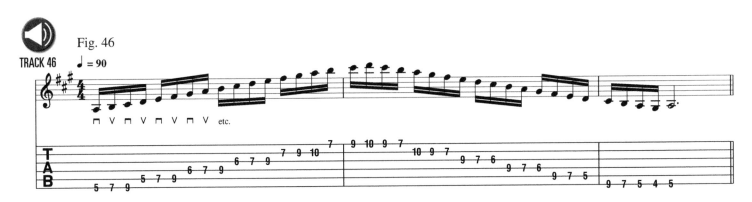

Fig. 46

TRACK 46 ♩ = 90

This example may give you some trouble—at first. Once the technique is mastered, however, you'll be ready to tackle your Yngwie Malmsteen collection of guitar music. The next example mixes it up a little bit, with two, three, and four notes per string as well as some nifty position shifting. Again, take your time, and concentrate on *strict* alternate picking to play the part.

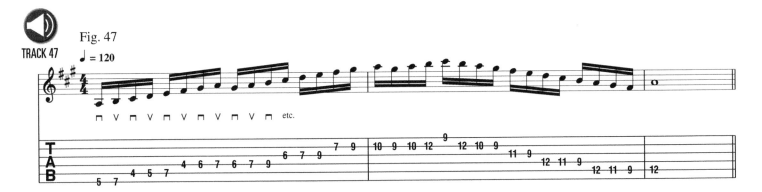

Fig. 47

TRACK 47 ♩ = 120

## Sweep Picking

I'm sorry to do this to you, but this next technique is completely opposite of what you just learned in alternate picking. *Sweep picking* gets its name from the "sweeping" motion of the pick hand when using the technique. It is most commonly used for arpeggios and is actually very similar to strumming, except that each note is articulated separately. So, rather than holding your fingers in place on the chord shape, you lift each one immediately after striking the note so it's not allowed to ring out. The first example uses only one-octave arpeggios crossing three strings. To get you into that neoclassical shred frame of mind, I've chosen a series of diminished 7th arpeggios that climb up the fretboard à la Yngwie Malmsteen.

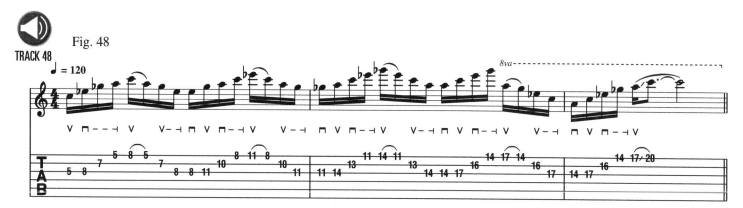

This next example stretches the arpeggios to cover between one-and-a-half and two-and-a-half octaves, complete with positional shifts on the neck to play the inversions as well. This exercise requires even greater precision and coordination between the hands, so work slowly. You should notice that the shapes of these arpeggios are based on barre chord forms with slight embellishments. This tidbit of knowledge should help you with fingering the argeggio.

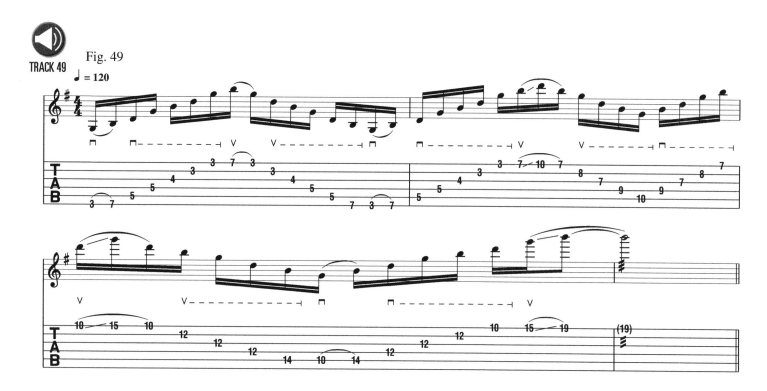

## Economy Picking

"OK, so for single-note lines, I should use alternate picking. And for arpeggios, I should try sweep picking. What if the music I'm playing contains both single-note lines and arpeggios?" Good question. Thankfully, there's an easy answer: Combine them! The merging of alternate picking and sweep picking kind of gives you the benefits of each, and it's name is *economy picking*.

As its name implies, economy picking is more economic in terms of movement. Basically a variation of alternate picking, economy picking lives by the same rules, but whenever you move from one string to another, you pick in the direction of the physical movement. So, where you used an upstroke to move from string 6 to string 5 in three-note-per-string alternate picking, you'd use a downstroke with economy picking.

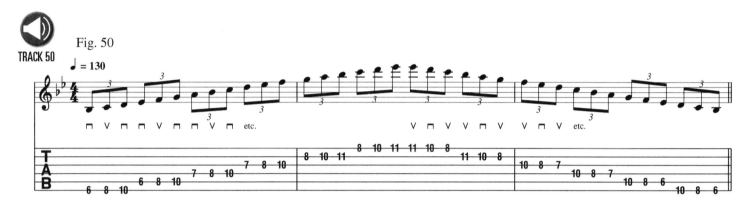

While this technique *is* more economical in terms of movement, it is usually not recommended to replace strict alternate picking in single note lines. Again, a strong command of strict alternate picking is beneficial for feeling the rhythm and maintaining the flow of the line. Economy picking does have its place, however, and it's in that combination of single-note lines and arpeggios. Try the example below first using strict alternate picking—even for the arpeggios. Then, repeat the passage using the indicated picking directions (between the notation staff and tab).

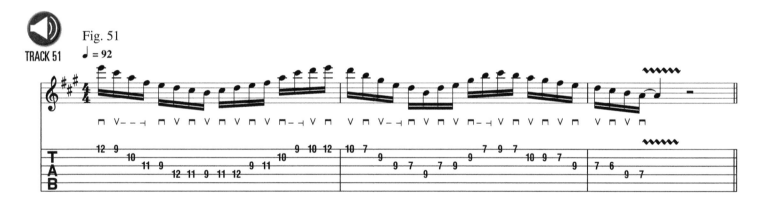

Which was easier? If you didn't notice a difference, increase the tempo and try both again. You should have felt more comfortable using economy picking for this example. If, however, you felt more comfortable using strict alternate picking, feel free to go with it. Ultimately, it all boils down to you making good music, so use whichever technique best helps you achieve that goal.

## Hybrid Picking

Now that you're fairly comfortable with both fingerpicking and flatpicking, why not combine those two techniques. *Hybrid picking* offers the best of both worlds—the flexibility and intervallic possibilities of fingerpicking and the strumming and speed aspects of the flatpick—in one handy-dandy package.

Hybrid picking allows the flatpicker to mingle chords and single-note lines without having to palm the pick, or worse yet, repeatedly insert and remove the pick from between your lips (which of course is *totally* out of the question if you sing while playing)! Holding the pick between your thumb and index finger as you normally would, the middle, ring, and pinky fingers are free to pluck chords, arpeggios, and embellishments as needed. This is especially popular in the jazz idiom, where flatpicking is typically desired for single-note lines, but the warmer, pianistic character of plucking chords is often preferred over strumming.

Practice using all three of your remaining fingers (middle, ring, and pinky) to pluck the treble strings. In the example below, there are five chords on which you can try this new technique. Conveniently, the notes fall on strings 4, 3, and 2, so you can assign each of your fingers to one of the strings and play the bass note with your pick.

For extra practice building the dexterity in your middle, ring, and pinky fingers, try playing the melodic lines beween the chords with your fingers as well as the pick

Fig. 52

TRACK 52

Jazz isn't the only place you'll find hybrid picking useful. High-speed, wide-interval lines, such as in the pedal-point example below, can also benefit from the hybrid treatment, as do banjo-style lines in country music. For this type of application, you'll generally use the flatpick in combination with either your middle or ring finger. Whichever you choose to use is largely based on your comfort level. Use the finger that feels most natural to you.

Try the following pedal point lines with alternate picking and then with hybrid picking. You should notice an immediate difference. Start slowly and work your way up to the tempo indicated.

Fig. 53

TRACK 53

**Chicken Pickin'**

Finally, you may have heard yet another variation of hybrid picking in your musical travels—this one from the country realm. By adding some "pop" to the strings that you pluck with your fingers, you get a technique known as *chicken pickin'*. One of the innovators of this technique was Don Rich, who was the guitarist for country legend Buck Owens. Using a twangy Tele, Rich would pluck the strings so hard you could hear them slap back against the guitar neck. Combined with rapid-fire guitar parts, this creates a "stuttering" sound effect.

In Fig. 54, use your pick to play the open A string and your fingers to pluck the double stops. In measure 4, use your pick to play the notes on the third string and pluck the first string with your ring finger. Be sure to hit the ghost notes for the stuttering sound, and remember to pluck hard enough to get the chicken pickin' tone!

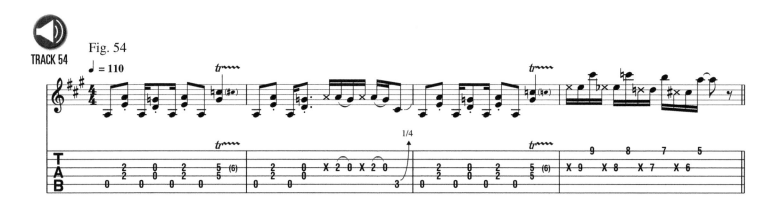

# TWO-HAND TAPPING

In the mid to late '70s, a new young rock guitarist was tearing up the Los Angeles club scene, playing guitar solos with two hands on the fretboard. Though this two-hand technique had been done before, this young man's flair, combined with changing musical times, was what it took to make other guitarists and fans take notice of the unusual technique. His name: Eddie Van Halen.

Others have found success using two-hand tapping extensively in their repertoire, including Stanley Jordan, Steve Vai, and Joe Satriani. Essentially, *tapping* is a hammer-on performed with one or more fingers on your pick hand. And as with the hammer-on technique discussed earlier, tapping is often used in conjunction with pull-offs (and slides) to keep the line moving. Tapping is considered a legato technique, and can be equally effective in scalar, arpeggio, and chordal contexts.

### One Finger Tapping

We'll start with the simplest tapping technique, and that's a one-finger hammer-on. Right off, you're faced with a bit of a decision: which finger to use. Either your index finger or your middle finger are acceptable; however, mastery of both is preferable.

Let's start with using your index finger. The biggest advantage of using the index finger is the extra control it affords. The index finger is simply used more often for a greater number of daily tasks, and therefore it is typically more "obedient" than the remaining fingers. Also, using the index finger allows you to use your thumb for support on the top edge of the fingerboard.

Now, you may be wondering: If you choose to use your index finger, and you play with a pick, what do you do with the pick? Try wedging it in the joints of your middle finger, or use your middle finger to hold it against your palm as in this photo.

Alternatively, you may choose to leave the pick right where you normally hold it between your thumb and index finger and instead use your middle finger to perform the tapping. If you're switching quickly between flatpicking and tapping, this is the preferred variation. It may take a little more getting used to however, as you will likely be a bit unsteady because your thumb is unable to support the position.

For starters, let's try tapping on the high E string with absolutely no left-hand involvement. When you tap onto the string, treat it in the same manner as fretting a note: Your tapping finger should hit the string just forward of the midpoint between the frets. This exercise also requires you to pull-off with your pick-hand finger in the same manner that you performed pull-offs with your fret hand. Play the example twice, once with your index finger, and once with your middle finger.

Fig. 55
TRACK 55    ♩ = 160

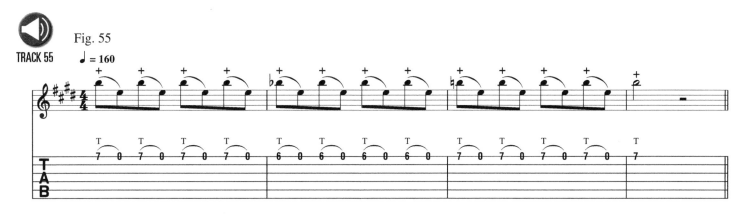

Now, let's add a note with your fret hand. First, perform the tap-on, then pull off to the open string, and follow that with a fret-hand hammer-on.

Fig. 56
TRACK 56    ♩ = 240

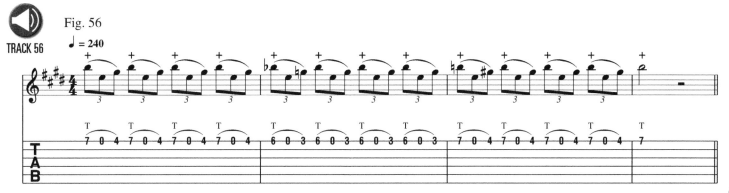

## Arpeggios

When we discussed arpeggios in the sweep picking section, they were laid out across the strings on the fretboard. Alternatively, you can use two-hand tapping to perform arpeggios on a single string – a much easier task. In fact, that's exactly what you did in Fig. 56. See how easy this is? You're already tapping into the two-handed arpeggio realm.

Tapped arpeggios offer a distinct sound from their sweep-picked cousins. Because tapping is a legato technique, it results in a much more fluid tone with typically better defined notes.

In the previous examples, you pulled off to open strings; however, you will also be required to pull off to fretted notes in real musical situations. In these cases, your fret-hand index finger usually becomes the anchor. Whatever the case, work on achieving a seamless, balanced attack with the taps, hammer-ons, and pull-offs. Let's tap into a few of these possibilities.

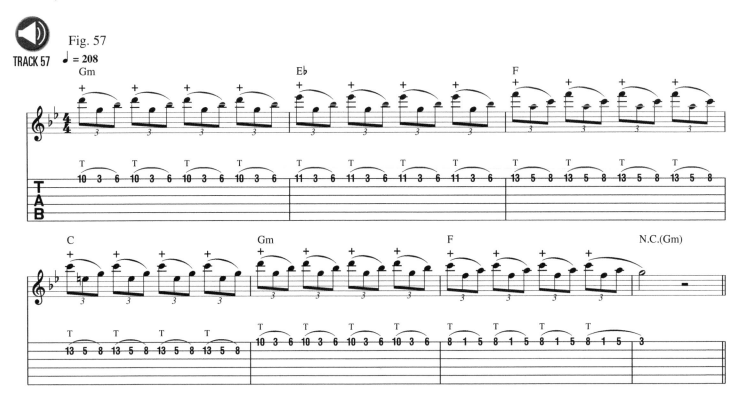

Some of you may now be asking, "What if I want to play more than one-octave arpeggios?" Those too can be played with a tapping technique, but require an extra dose of dexterity and patience. As you will soon see, two-octave (or more) arpeggios are played on more than one string, often include additional scale tones, and typically require you to skip to a nonadjacent string. The key is to take your time and play them cleanly before trying to increase the tempo.

Fig. 58

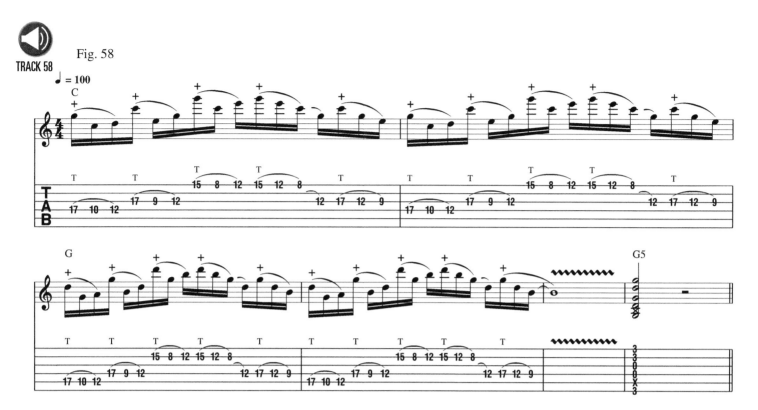

Finally, you can combine sweep picking with tapping to further extend your arpeggios, too. The key to performing this tricky technique is proper positioning of the pick hand. For example, in the musical figure below, you're sweep picking an E major arpeggio at the fourth fret, hammering on the B note with your fret-hand pinky finger, and then tapping the E note at the twelfth fret. If you perform the sweep picking portion with your pick hand over the guitar's pickups (which is where your pick hand normally attacks the strings), you've got a long way to move your hand to tap onto the twelfth fret. Since this technique is usually performed as part of a fast-moving line, your chance of error is greatly increased. If, however, you perform the sweep picking portion over the neck (approximately the fifteenth fret), your tapping finger will be in an advantageous position for the tapped E note.

Fig. 59

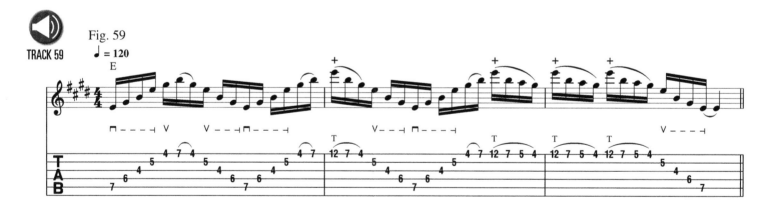

## Scalar Sequences

Tapping is by no means limited to use with arpeggios. The technique is very effective for extending scalar legato lines, too. To get you started, let's begin by using only one finger on the pick hand to add some life to a pentatonic minor scale pattern.

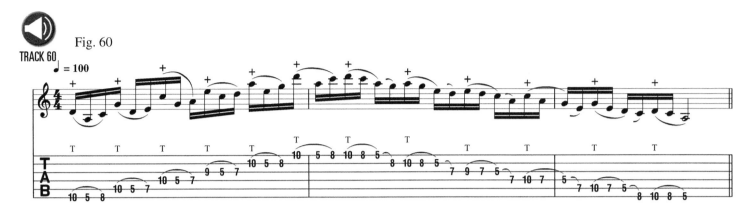

Fig. 60

TRACK 60 ♩ = 100

More commonly, this type of tapping technique is used in conjunction with three-note-per-string scale patterns to create searing legato lines.

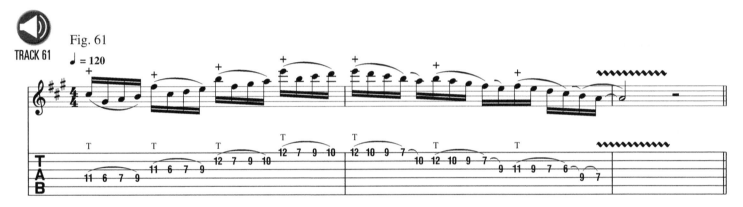

Fig. 61

TRACK 61 ♩ = 120

## Tap and Slide

By incorporating other fret-hand legato techniques such as *slides,* into your pick-hand bag of tricks, you can take your newfound ferocious tapping technique to even greater levels. One of the most prominent guitarists to preach the "tap and slide" gospel was George Lynch. A tremendous legato player, it didn't take long for Lynch to take his already formidable technique up a notch or two by tapping and sliding his way around the fretboard.

To perform the tap and slide technique, simply tap onto the note with your preferred pick-hand finger, and while maintaining pressure on the note, slide it toward the bridge to raise the pitch, or toward the nut to lower the pitch. Once you reach your target note, you have another decision to make. You can either pull off to an open string or fretted note, or you can slide to another position. The possibilities are limited only by your musical imagination.

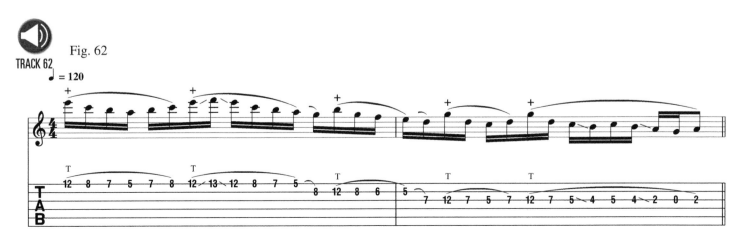

Fig. 62

TRACK 62 ♩ = 120

Now, if you're really feeling up for a challenge, let's try combining sweep picking with legato scalar sequencing and the tap and slide technique. Earlier, we combined sweep picking with tapping, so you're simply repeating that exercise with a few additional notes and a slide.

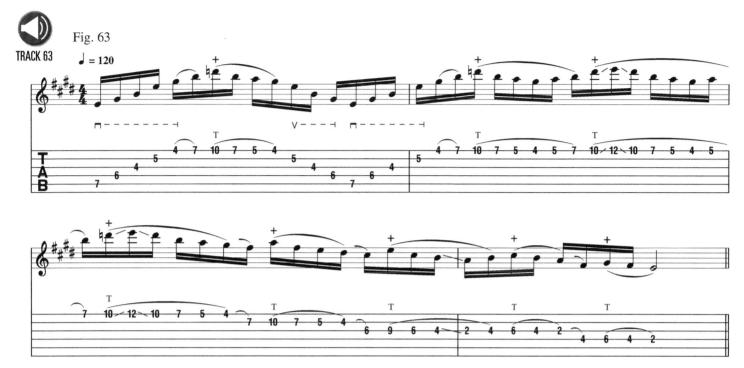

Fig. 63

TRACK 63    ♩ = 120

## Multifinger Tapping

Eight notes in a major scale from root through octave, and eight fingers on two human hands (not including thumbs)—coincidence? Back in the mid '80s, Steve Lynch (Autograph) and Jeff Watson (Night Ranger) made a lot of noise—and notes—via their amazing eight-finger tapping techniques. Though the moniker was more symbolic than definitive, as all eight fingers were rarely used in a single line, both players routinely recruited five or six fingers to play their legendary legato lines.

To perform multifinger tapping, you'll first need to "lose" your pick. If you have a pick holder on your guitar or mic stand, that will work fine. Otherwise, you can do it the old-fashioned way—put it in your mouth (please don't choke!). Your fret hand is positioned normally, but your pick hand should be above the neck, opposite the fret hand. In this manner, you can tap onto the strings piano-style with your right hand. You'll want to place your pick-hand thumb on the top edge of the neck, slightly toward the underside, to offer your hand support and stability.

Let's start with a D major arpeggio that uses an open string (D) and two fingers from each hand. Concentrate on achieving equal volume with each hammer-on and pull-off.

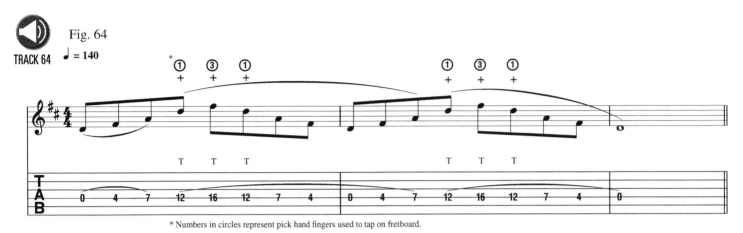

Fig. 64
TRACK 64  ♩ = 140

* Numbers in circles represent pick hand fingers used to tap on fretboard.

Now, let's incorporate some scale tones and extend the lines to require three and four fingers from the pick hand. Remember, your attacks should be balanced, and it's going to take some practice to get that high E note to ring with authority when tapping with your pick-hand pinky finger. Take it slow and work hard to keep it clean. Once you've got this example down, try switching to other strings or incorporating this type of line into a normally picked solo.

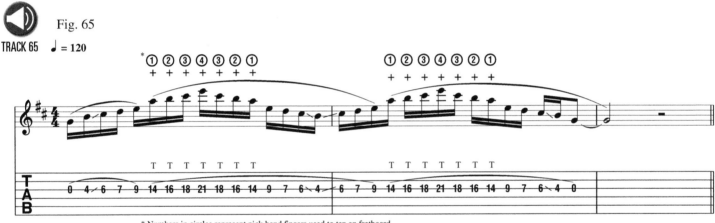

Fig. 65
TRACK 65  ♩ = 120

* Numbers in circles represent pick hand fingers used to tap on fretboard.

### Chordal Tapping

And you thought the tapping section ended with that last bonanza, didn't you? Thus far, we've focused on the tapping technique as it's used to produce melodies and arpeggios. However, it is quite effective for producing chords as well. Jazz maestro Stanley Jordan is the king of the chordal tapping, and one of the reasons his music is so interesting is the pianistic, wide-interval voicings he can achieve by playing chords in this manner.

As with the tapping techniques discussed previously, the chordal tapping technique is performed with pick-hand hammer-ons. Whereas before you hammered onto a single string, the chordal tapping technique requires you to attack several strings, either at once, or in an arpeggiated fashion.

Typically, any notes located toward the nut will be hammered on with your fret hand, and the notes toward the bridge will be hammered with your pick hand. A key concern in executing this type of attack is that you need to be mindful of accidental muting. Since you may have anywhere between three and six strings ringing at once, you must be quite precise in your attack. Let's start with some triads and dominant chords.

Fig. 66

TRACK 66   ♩ = 80

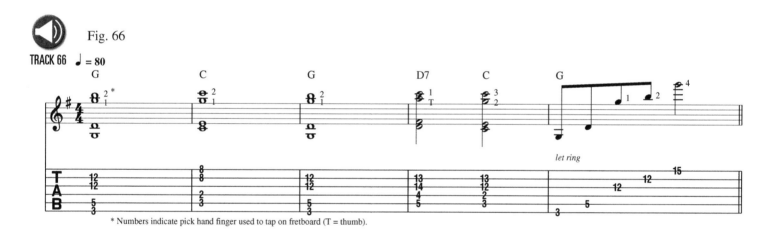

* Numbers indicate pick hand finger used to tap on fretboard (T = thumb).

Now, let's syncopate the rhythm a little bit to create the illusion of two instruments (bass and guitar) playing at the same time.

Fig. 67

TRACK 67   ♩ = 60

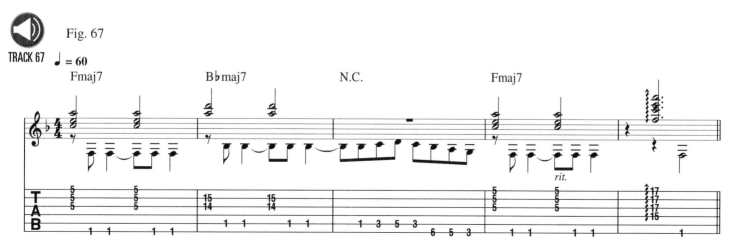

# ARTIFICIAL HARMONICS

In the first half of *Guitar Techniques*, we discussed naturally occuring harmonics on the open strings. The same physics principles that govern those harmonics can be applied to fretted notes as well. When you fret a note on the fingerboard, you're essentially changing the functional length of the string. That fretted note becomes the fundamental, and further subdivisions of the new string length will produce harmonics of that fundamental tone. Here's a table showing the location of artificial harmonics.

| Fundamental | fretted note |
| --- | --- |
| 1st Harmonic | 12 frets from fretted note |
| 2nd Harmonic | 7 or 19 frets from fretted note |
| 3rd Harmonic | 5 frets from fretted note |

### Tap Harmonics

There are several ways to produce these harmonics, and they all involve the pick hand. The first of these techniques is termed *tap harmonics*. This variation requires you to tap directly onto a designated fret with one of your pick-hand fingers. The tap should be on the fretwire itself, rather than between the frets. The same relative physical locations apply here as they did with natural harmonics. Referring back to that unit, you'll remember that dividing the length of the string in half was achieved by forcing a node at the twelfth fret—twelve frets above the fundamental pitch. Same goes for a fretted pitch. Say, for example, you're fretting the A note at the fifth fret on the sixth string. To play the first harmonic, tap onto the string twelve frets higher than the fretted pitch (seventeenth fret). This should've produced an A note, one octave higher. Let's try this with an entire A major barre chord at the fifth fret. The tapped notes are in parentheses next to the fretted notes on the tab staff. Use either your index or middle finger to tap onto the frets.

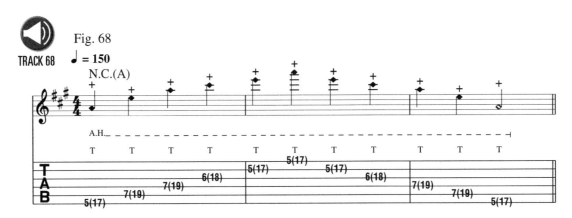

Fig. 68
TRACK 68 ♩ = 150

Each of the tones you produced sounded exactly one octave higher than the fretted notes. Now, try the exercise again but this time, you'll be tapping seven frets higher than the fretted pitch, which will produce tones an octave plus a perfect 5th above the fundamental.

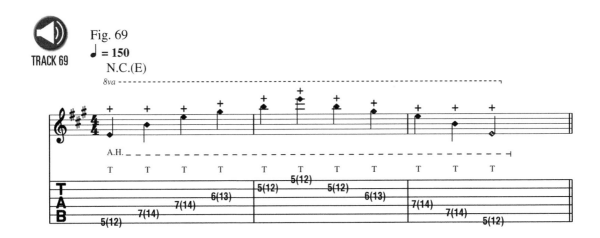

Fig. 69
TRACK 69 ♩ = 150

Try repeating the exercise tapping five frets above the fundamental, which produces harmonics two octaves above the fretted pitch.

After you've done that, try your hand at the lead guitar lick below designed to tap into your newfound skills.

Fig. 70

TRACK 70 ♩ = 120

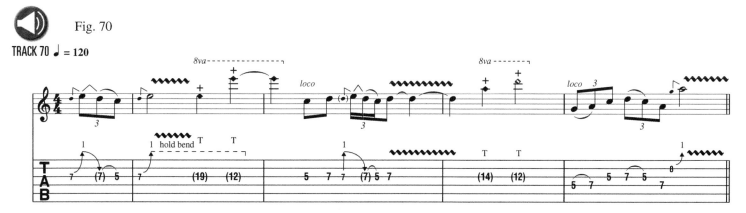

## Harp Harmonics

A technique similar to tap harmonics that has a cleaner (but somewhat more difficult) attack is called *harp harmonics*. In this technique, rather than tapping onto the fret and string, the pick hand lightly touches the string over the designated fret in the same manner as the fret hand for natural harmonics. Then, you use another pick-hand finger or a flatpick to pluck the string and sound the harmonic. If you're playing fingerstyle, fret the harmonic with your pick-hand index finger, and pluck the string with your thumb or one of your remaining fingers.

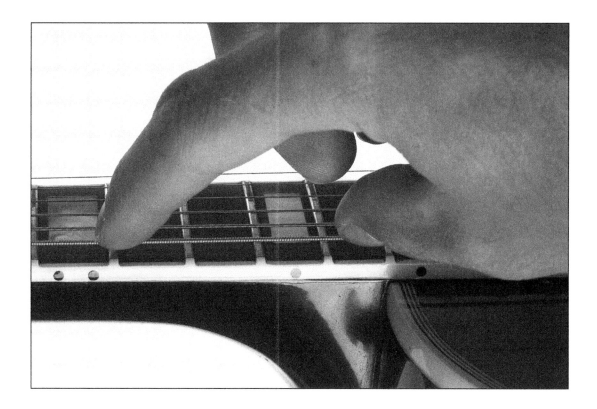

If you wish to use a flatpick (recommended if you normally play with one), hold the pick between your thumb and *middle* finger, and use your index finger to lightly touch the string over the appropriate frets.

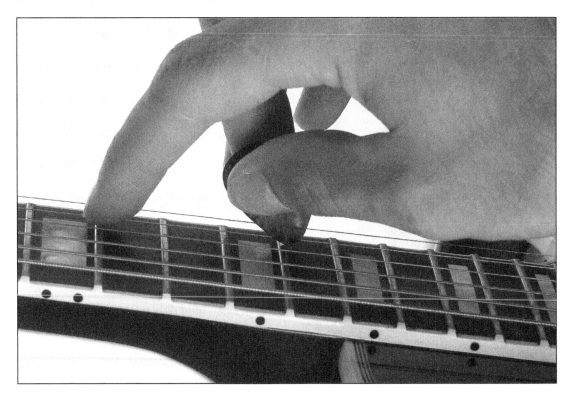

For a warmup, let's try a G major barre chord at the 3rd fret, playing harmonics one octave (twelve frets) higher.

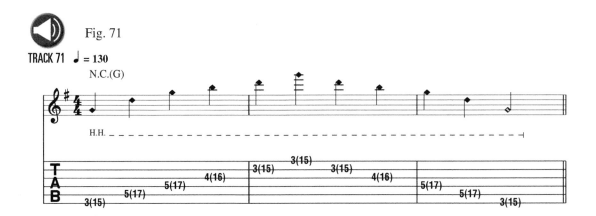

Fig. 71

TRACK 71 ♩ = 130

Like the tap harmonics previously, let's produce both the second (seven frets above) and third (five frets above) harmonics of the G major chord, too.

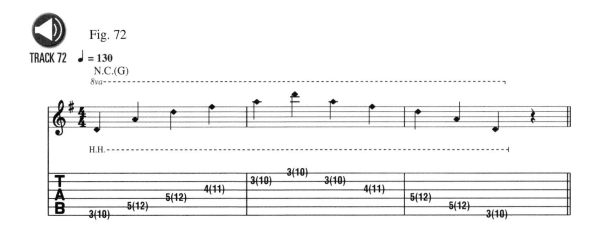

Fig. 72

TRACK 72 ♩ = 130

Whereas tap harmonics work really well within a soloing context, harp harmonics not only fulfill the same role, they are also incredibly effective composition tools, particularly when mixed in with arpeggios to create cascading harp-like sounds. To hear masters of harp harmonics at work, check out the fancy fretting of Lenny Breau, Ted Greene, or Eric Johnson.

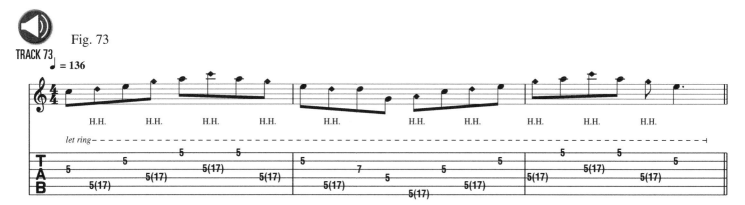

Fig. 73

TRACK 73

## Pinch Harmonics

The final harmonic technique that you need to be familiar with is called *pinch harmonics*. To produce a pinch harmonic correctly, you simultaneously attack the string with either a flatpick or a fingernail from your pick hand and lightly touch the string with the side of your pick-hand thumb.

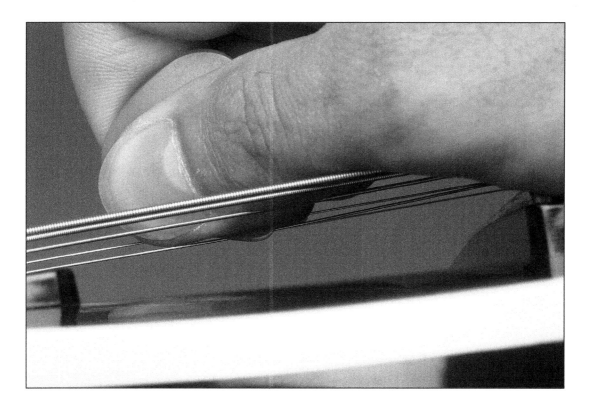

The spot that your thumb was touching when the string was struck is not allowed to ring, thus creating a node, which divides the string into two vibrating sections thereby sounding a higher harmonic of the fretted note. This technique works on any open string or fretted note, and the harmonic produced also depends on where you attack the string with your pick hand, so experiment with producing different harmonics of the same fretted pitch.

Some fret-hand vibrato and a little (or a lot) of distortion will help the quieter harmonic come to life. This particular technique became a symbolic sound of '80s metal guitar, and was perhaps most popularized by former Ozzy Osbourne guitarist Zakk Wylde. His tonally lethal combination of high gain amps, active pickups, and the forever-sustaining Gibson Les Paul provided the perfect recipe for screeching harmonic mayhem. Try the example below with your distortion cranked way up.

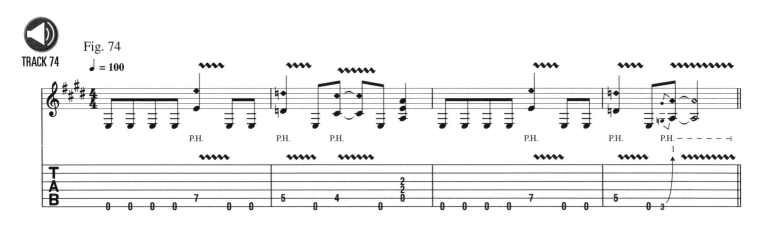

TRACK 74

Fig. 74

## WHAMMY BAR

Many electric guitars come with a funky little attachment called the *whammy bar*, also known as a tremolo system. One listen to an early Steve Vai or Joe Satriani album will quickly make you aware of just what can be done with this magical little bar. The basic structure of a tremolo system consists of a metal arm that attaches to the bridge, which is fastened to a set of springs in the back of the guitar's body, thus allowing the user to manipulate string tension resulting in a change of pitch.

There are two main types of whammy bars: standard and floating. The standard tremolo system only allows you to lower the pitch of the strings by decreasing the tension. As you press down on the bar, the string tension slackens, thus lowering the pitch. In its resting position, the bridge rests against the guitar body, so pulling up on the bar to increase tension and pitch is impossible.

If you wish to raise the pitch of a note via the whammy bar, you need a floating tremolo system, the most popular of which is the Floyd Rose. Floating tremolo systems allow you to pull up on the bar, limited only by string tension. With some systems, it's possible to produce a range of pitch variation from completely slack to three whole steps above the fundamental pitch.

## Whammy Bar Vibrato

Whammy bar use is not limited only to dramatic octave-plus pitch fluctuations. The fret-hand vibrato techniques we covered earlier can be replicated using a whammy bar, too. If you'll remember, we said that classical-style vibrato (parallel to the string) was the only fret-hand vibrato technique that can both raise *and* lower the pitch. That's true, but with a floating tremolo system, you can produce the same effect with a whammy bar. Since the classical-style vibrato is a very subtle effect, it will take great patience and control to emulate it with a bar, as the tendency is to over-vibrato with a whammy bar. In the next example, use very little force as you depress and pull up on the whammy bar to produce the vibrato.

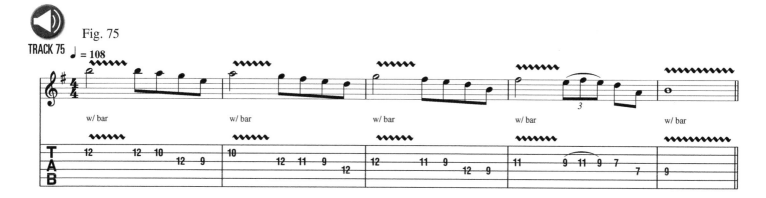

This next whammy bar technique will be very simple compared to the last one. In this next example, you should try to emulate both a normal pivot vibrato and a wide, dramatic vibrato using the bar.

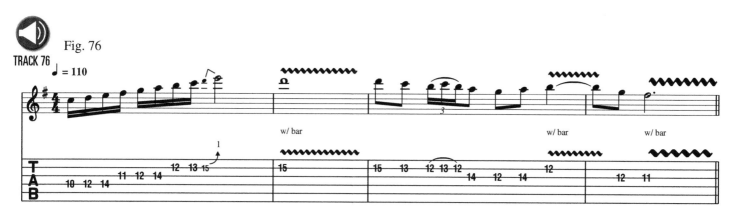

## Whammy Bar Bends

In addition to vibrato, you can also execute bends using the bar instead of your fret-hand fingers. This is a very simple technique: Simply play the desired note, grab the bar, and pull up on it until you reach your target pitch. Like bending with the fingers, this may take some time to consistently achieve proper intonation. To get started, play the note from which you're starting the bend. Then play the note that you wish to bend up to. Next, play the first note again and execute the bend with the bar, matching the fretted target note. Try this with half-, whole-, and greater bends. One word of caution, however, don't pull up too hard, or you may be spending more time replacing broken strings than practicing.

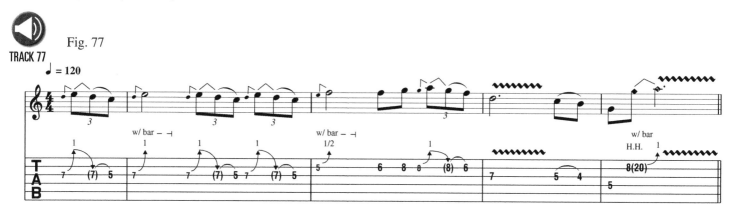

## Whammy Bar Scoops and Dips

One of the many cool tricks you can employ with a whammy bar is called a *scoop*. The scoop produces a "notes from nowhere" type of sound, similar to a slide. It's typically a fairly aggressive technique, so don't be shy. To use the scoop technique, first depress the bar until the strings are nearly slack. Then hammer on the desired fretted pitch, quickly following that up with a rapid release of the whammy bar.

*Note that you do not raise the pitch above that of the fretted note; simply raise the bar back to its resting position.

Another whammy technique, which is kind of a mix of vibrato and scoop, is called the dip. The dip consists of a rapid depression from and return to a fretted pitch. It is important to note that dips typically have a controlled, consistent fluctuation; they are not random. Feel free to perform this technique slower than normal to become familiar with how much force is needed to depress the bar for a half- or a whole-step dip.

Dips tend to work well with long, sustained notes, especially in a rock or metal format. The example below contains a series of scoops leading to whole-step dips in a rock guitar context. The key is to accurately hit the whole-step depression in the rapid manner required for the right effect.

TRACK 78  Fig. 78  ♩ = 140

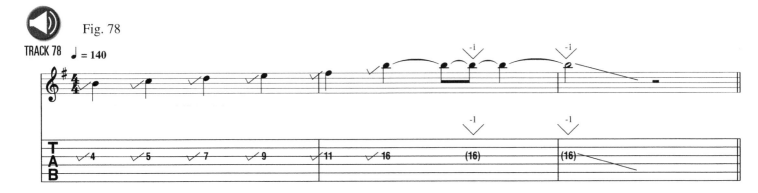

## Extreme Whammy Bar

And now the fun begins. Let's face it, although the whammy bar is useful for producing basic effects such as vibrato and unique effects like scoops and dips, once it's in your hands, you want to go crazy with it. Let's begin with a technique that anyone can do with a whammy bar, regardless of the tremolo system on your guitar.

The *divebomb* is just what it sounds like. We'll begin with an open string. (Note: This sounds best when used with gobs of distortion!) Strike the open low E string, grab the whammy bar, and depress it until the E string is slack and flopping around. Hold it in that position for a second or two, and then slowly release the bar back to its resting position. One option with this technique is to pluck the string with your fret-hand fingers while it is slack thus producing an odd rumbling-like noise. Alternatively, you may simply choose to mute the string once it's reached a slack condition. Let's incorporate this cool technique into a heavy rock riff.

TRACK 79  Fig. 79  ♩ = 100

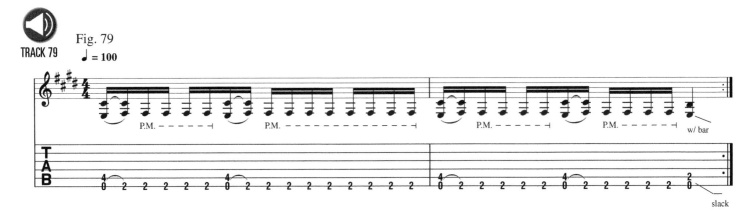

The polar opposite of the divebomb, and often used in conjunction with it, is the screeching high note—typically a harmonic of some sort. Moving from the sonic depths to stratospheric frequencies has long been a staple crowd-pleaser for rock guitarists. You've already mastered the first half of this trick with the divebomb, so let's focus on reaching new heights at the brink of string breakage! For this section, you'll need a floating tremolo system that allows you to raise the pitch by pulling up on the bar.

In previous lessons and on your own, I'm sure, you've discovered how far you're willing to pull up on the whammy bar for fear of breaking a string. In this next exercise, we'll work our way up the tension ladder to the point at which string manufacturers begin saying, "A little further, now."

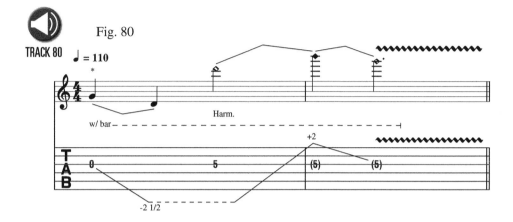

To produce *really* high notes, you can apply the whammy bar to a second or third harmonic. For instance, the third harmonic of the open E string is an E note two octaves higher than the fundamental. Take that note up an additional 1½ steps and it's like you're playing a note at the twenty-seventh fret. Try bending the high E string on a standard twenty-two-fret neck to reach that note!

Now, let's combine divebombs with screeching harmonics to produce a cliché cap to the standard hard rock guitar solo.

**Whammy Bar Flutter**

One final whammy technique, called the *flutter technique*, produces a "chirping-like" sound and is especially popular in hard rock and heavy metal music. To pull it off, start by trilling between two notes with your fret hand. Then, slightly depress the whammy bar with the middle and ring fingers of your pick hand, allowing them to "slip off" the bar so that the bar "snaps" back to resting position. This will cause the springs of the tremolo system to vibrate rapidly, which in turn causes tiny, ultra-rapid pitch fluctuations and a warbling- or chirp-like sound. It works either with or without distortion, but sounds best with gobs of gain.

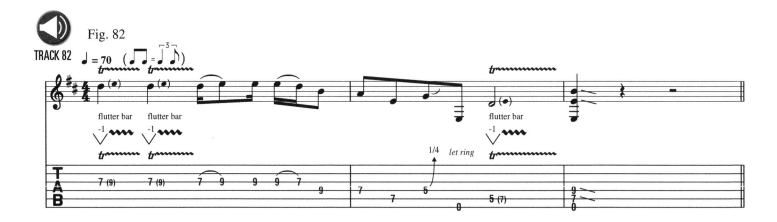

# MISCELLANEOUS TECHNIQUES

The techniques presented thus far pretty much cover all the bases in a standard repertoire, but there are countless others that could be covered. To wrap things up, I'm dedicating these last few pages to a few select tricks that players have developed over the years.

# BENDING/VIBRATO

Just when you thought you've had all the vibrato one can take, we shake things up a bit further. The techniques I'm about to discuss are functionally closer to whammy bar substitutes than vibrato techniques, but this is their true umbrella category.

Depending on the type of guitar you play, there are up to three more ways to change the pitch of a ringing note. If you have a standard nut on your guitar (not locking), pushing down on the string behind the nut will raise the pitch of a note played on that string. This technique requires some heavy-duty toughening of your fingertips, but it's a great way to bend or apply vibrato to a harmonic when you don't have a whammy bar at your disposal.

Fig. 83

TRACK 83 ♩ = 100

* Bend by pushing on string behind the nut.

** Vibrato applied by pushing on strings behind the nut.

Similarly, you can also push down on the string between the bridge and tailpiece (on a Gibson Les Paul, for example) to produce the same effect. This, however, is quite difficult in terms of strength and the pressure on your fingertips. Try using the side edge of your pick if you attempt this trick.

Finally, you can change the pitch of a note by—are you sitting down?—*bending* the neck itself! This is a technique that I present to you with much caution. It is to be done *very* carefully, as too much force can snap the neck. Wood is somewhat elastic, which means it can be bent and will return to shape (within limits), thus making this technique possible. I've frequently seen it employed by both bass players and acoustic guitarists.

Let's try this technique with natural harmonics. Play the harmonics at the twelfth fret on the open second and first strings. While the note is ringing, place your pick hand on the upper bout of your guitar, and your fret hand behind the neck, where the fingerboard meets the headstock. Push gently with both hands, thus causing a slight concave curvature to the neck, which in turn slackens the strings and lowers the pitch. Release the force, and the string tension returns to normal. To put it into a musical context, try the lick below.

Fig. 84

TRACK 84 ♩ = 120

* Bend produced by bending the neck

# VOLUME SWELLS

One of the many cool yet under-appreciated features of an electric guitar is the ability to control volume *after* the string attack. For example, if you attack the string with the volume off and subsequently turn it up, you've just performed a *volume swell*. This technique produces an almost violin-like tonal quality. There are two ways to perform volume swells: with the guitar's volume knob or with a volume pedal.

Volume knob manipulation is more common because you don't need to purchase an additional piece of equipment, but it also

requires a bit more dexterity when performing fast lines. Guitars such as the Fender Strat have their volume knobs placed very near the bridge pickup, which allows the player to curl his or her pinky finger around the knob while playing to facilitate rapidly played passages.

Rather than picking the notes, you may wish to use hammer-ons, which will enable you to focus your pick hand entirely on the volume knob.

Neoclassical rock guitar virtuoso Yngwie Malmsteen is one master of this deft technique. And when he combines volume swells with classically inspired melody lines, the technique is that much more effective. Give this neoclassical notefest a whirl using the volume knob to produce the swells. Remember, attack the note with the volume rolled off, quickly turn the volume knob on with your pinky finger, and then roll it off again before striking the next note. To make this line extra-special, add an echo delay set to repeat between notes.

If you have a volume pedal among your effects, it may provide a simpler alternative to volume knob manipulation. Try the above example again, this time using a volume pedal. Perhaps the most common use for volume swells is to creat ambient, sonic textures. This is especially effective when used with chord.

For the next example, you can use either the volume knob or a pedal. Strum the chord with the volume off, then turn the volume on at a moderate pace. Remember to turn the volume off again before switching chords.

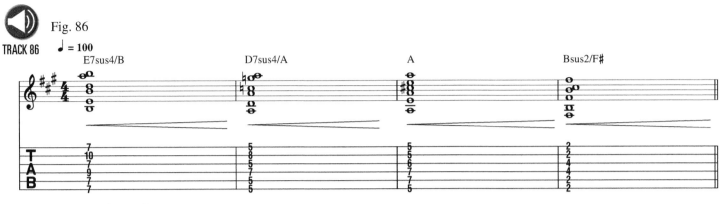

## KOTO PICKING

The unusual *Koto* technique is so named because the sound mimics that of the Japanese Koto, an instrument with seven to thirteen silk strings that are plucked by the fingers. Koto picking is not that difficult to master, as it simply requires you to attack the strings very near to where they're fretted. For example, if you're playing a C note fretted on the third string at the fifth fret, pick the string at the seventh fret. You should hear a thin, brittle attack sound. If so, you're doing it right! This technique sounds best mixed in with bends and a touch of the Japanese major scale (1–♭2–4–5–♭6).

You can also achieve this effect by picking the strings right next to the bridge. This also gets that thin, brittle sound—and it's a little easier!

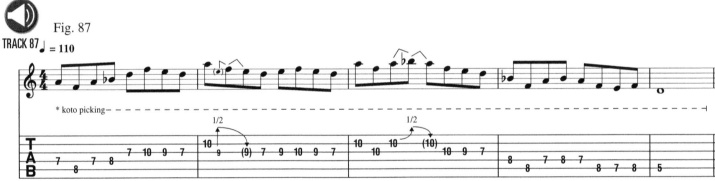

* Pick string within 3 frets of the fretted note.

## PICK SCRAPES

Long a staple of rock guitar, the *pick scrape* has a very unique and rather undefinable sound. Employed by scraping the edge of the pick along the length of the strings, it works best on wound strings (usually the fourth, fifth, and sixth strings). Moving from the bridge toward the nut, you can lead with either the thumb side of the pick or the index finger side of the pick, whichever is more comfortable for you.

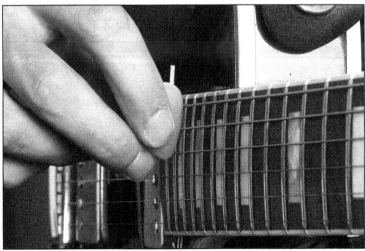

Eddie Van Halen is one of the most noted players to incorporate pick scrapes, as evidenced in the classic Van Halen version of "You Really Got Me." In that song, Eddie employs pick scrapes in the intro, in the beginning of the solo, at the end of the solo, and at the end of the song. These are the most common places to hear pick scrapes employed, and Eddie hits all of them. Try the Van Halen-esque rhythm guitar part below to get your pick-scrape chops up to par.

**TRACK 88**

Fig. 88

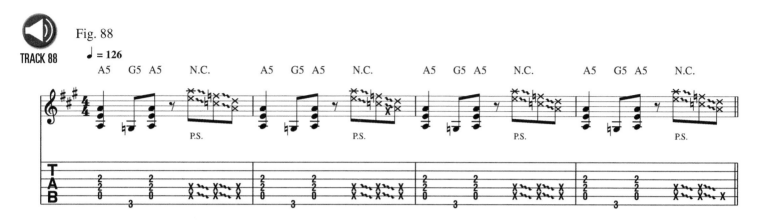

## PICKUP SELECTOR MANIPULATION

While we're discussing Van Halen's version of "You Really Got Me," this is as good a time as any to mention *pickup selector manipulation*. This technique only works on a guitar that has independent volume controls for each pickup (e.g., Gibson Les Paul). Essentially, you're performing "instantaneous volume swells" by switching from a pickup that's not producing any output to one with a live signal. To perform this technique, set the volume for one of your pickups to "10." Turn the other volume control all the way off. After striking a note or chord, quickly alternate between the two using the selector switch to produce a live signal. You should hear an "on/off" pattern of sound.

For more examples of what can be done with a pickup selector switch, check out Tom Morello's guitar work on Rage Against the Machine's self-titled debut album.

**TRACK 89**

Fig. 89

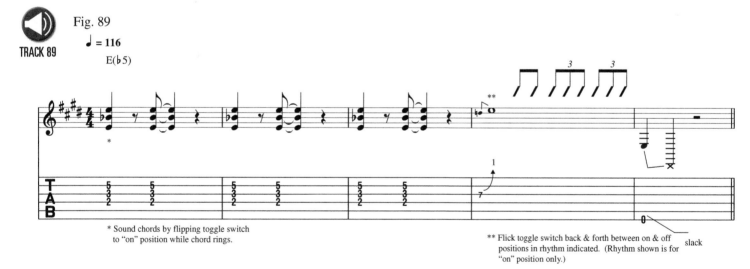

\* Sound chords by flipping toggle switch
to "on" position while chord rings.

\*\* Flick toggle switch back & forth between on & off
positions in rhythm indicated. (Rhythm shown is for
"on" position only.)

# SLAP AND POP

A popular technique among funk bassists, the *slap and pop* technique can be applied to guitar as well. Slap and pop is basically a variation of fingerstyle guitar, but instead of plucking bass strings with your thumb, you "slap" the string against the fretboard with the side of your thumb. For the remaining fingers, the plucking is altered by first pulling up on the string so that when it's released, it slams against the fingerboard causing a "popping" sound.

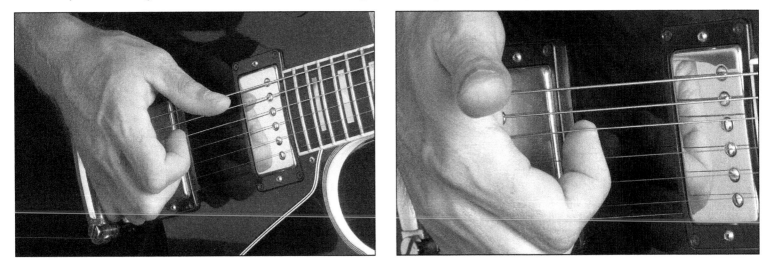

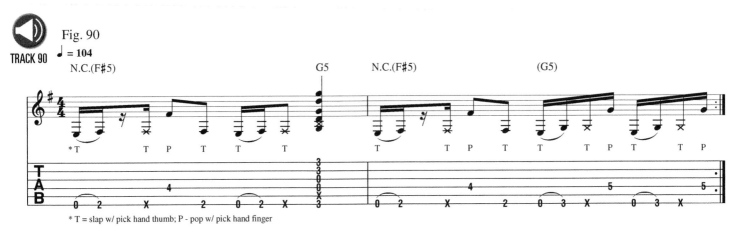

Fig. 90

TRACK 90  ♩ = 104

* T = slap w/ pick hand thumb; P - pop w/ pick hand finger

The technique isn't as eclectic as it may appear. Country and funk guitar players have long used the popping technique as a defining element in the classic twang and funk sound. A Tele- or Strat-style guitar is recommended for emulating this sound, with the pickup selector set out-of-phase between the middle and neck pickups. Try the "funky music" lick below and be sure to get those pops a-poppin'.

Fig. 91

TRACK 91  ♩ = 110

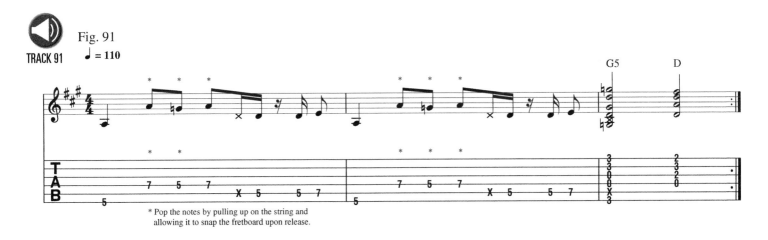

* Pop the notes by pulling up on the string and
  allowing it to snap the fretboard upon release.

# PLAYING WITH YOUR TEETH

To conclude *Guitar Techniques*, I feel it appropriate to present the "end-all, be-all" of show-off techniques guaranteed to make any crowd roar—*playing with your teeth*! First made popular by Jimi Hendrix, picking with teeth has probably since been attempted by every young, budding, rock-star guitarist to ever strap on an axe.

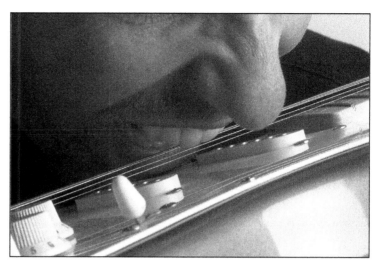

There's no real secret to playing with your teeth outside of developing good aiming skills. Take your time, and keep it simple. You won't be performing intricate improvisations in this manner, just a few notes to make the crowd erupt. Be careful, however, not to chip your teeth in the process by accidentally banging them into the guitar's body.

Fig. 92

TRACK 92 ♩ = 100

# CONCLUSION

There you have them. Fifty guitar techniques ranging from requisite to off-the-wall. I hope you've found this reference guide useful, and more importantly, I hope it sparked new musical ideas. Even if some of the techniques herein don't normally apply to your style of music, there are no rules that say you can't incorporate them anyway. Use them to strengthen and expand your musical foundation. Most of all, though, have fun. Happy pickin'.

# Guitar Notation Legend

Guitar music can be notated three different ways: on a *musical staff*, in *tablature*, and in *rhythm slashes*.

**RHYTHM SLASHES** are written above the staff. Strum chords in the rhythm indicated. Use the chord diagrams found at the top of the first page of the transcription for the appropriate chord voicings. Round noteheads indicate single notes.

**THE MUSICAL STAFF** shows pitches and rhythms and is divided by bar lines into measures. Pitches are named after the first seven letters of the alphabet.

**TABLATURE** graphically represents the guitar fingerboard. Each horizontal line represents a string, and each number represents a fret.

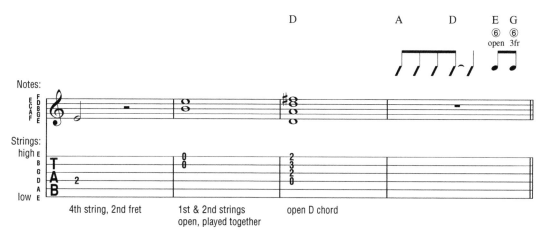

4th string, 2nd fret | 1st & 2nd strings open, played together | open D chord

# Definitions for Special Guitar Notation

**HALF-STEP BEND:** Strike the note and bend up 1/2 step.

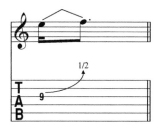

**WHOLE-STEP BEND:** Strike the note and bend up one step.

**GRACE NOTE BEND:** Strike the note and immediately bend up as indicated.

**SLIGHT (MICROTONE) BEND:** Strike the note and bend up 1/4 step.

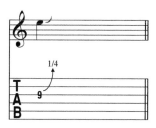

**BEND AND RELEASE:** Strike the note and bend up as indicated, then release back to the original note. Only the first note is struck.

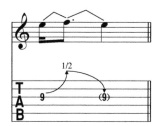

**PRE-BEND:** Bend the note as indicated, then strike it.

**PRE-BEND AND RELEASE:** Bend the note as indicated. Strike it and release the bend back to the original note.

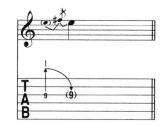

**UNISON BEND:** Strike the two notes simultaneously and bend the lower note up to the pitch of the higher.

**VIBRATO:** The string is vibrated by rapidly bending and releasing the note with the fretting hand.

**WIDE VIBRATO:** The pitch is varied to a greater degree by vibrating with the fretting hand.

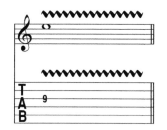

**HAMMER-ON:** Strike the first (lower) note with one finger, then sound the higher note (on the same string) with another finger by fretting it without picking.

**PULL-OFF:** Place both fingers on the notes to be sounded. Strike the first note and without picking, pull the finger off to sound the second (lower) note.

**LEGATO SLIDE:** Strike the first note and then slide the same fret-hand finger up or down to the second note. The second note is not struck.

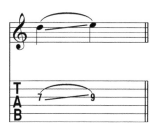

**SHIFT SLIDE:** Same as legato slide, except the second note is struck.

**TRILL:** Very rapidly alternate between the notes indicated by continuously hammering on and pulling off.

**TAPPING:** Hammer ("tap") the fret indicated with the pick-hand index or middle finger and pull off to the note fretted by the fret hand.

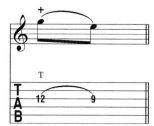

**NATURAL HARMONIC:** Strike the note while the fret-hand lightly touches the string directly over the fret indicated.

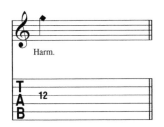

**PINCH HARMONIC:** The note is fretted normally and a harmonic is produced by adding the edge of the thumb or the tip of the index finger of the pick hand to the normal pick attack.

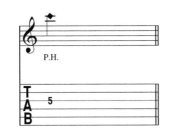

**HARP HARMONIC:** The note is fretted normally and a harmonic is produced by gently resting the pick hand's index finger directly above the indicated fret (in parentheses) while the pick hand's thumb or pick assists by plucking the appropriate string.

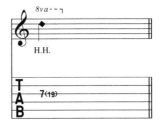

**PICK SCRAPE:** The edge of the pick is rubbed down (or up) the string, producing a scratchy sound.

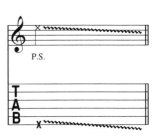

**MUFFLED STRINGS:** A percussive sound is produced by laying the fret hand across the string(s) without depressing, and striking them with the pick hand.

**PALM MUTING:** The note is partially muted by the pick hand lightly touching the string(s) just before the bridge.

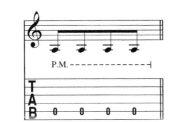

**RAKE:** Drag the pick across the strings indicated with a single motion.

**TREMOLO PICKING:** The note is picked as rapidly and continuously as possible.

**ARPEGGIATE:** Play the notes of the chord indicated by quickly rolling them from bottom to top.

**VIBRATO BAR DIVE AND RETURN:** The pitch of the note or chord is dropped a specified number of steps (in rhythm), then returned to the original pitch.

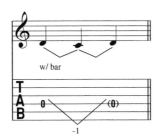

**VIBRATO BAR SCOOP:** Depress the bar just before striking the note, then quickly release the bar.

**VIBRATO BAR DIP:** Strike the note and then immediately drop a specified number of steps, then release back to the original pitch.

# Additional Musical Definitions

| | | |
|---|---|---|
| (accent) | • Accentuate note (play it louder). | |
| (accent) | • Accentuate note with great intensity. | |
| (staccato) | • Play the note short. | |
| ⊓ | • Downstroke | |
| V | • Upstroke | |

**D.S. al Coda** — • Go back to the sign ( 𝄋 ), then play until the measure marked "*To Coda*," then skip to the section labelled "**Coda**."

**D.C. al Fine** — • Go back to the beginning of the song and play until the measure marked "*Fine*" (end).

**Rhy. Fig.** — • Label used to recall a recurring accompaniment pattern (usually chordal).

**Riff** — • Label used to recall composed, melodic lines (usually single notes) which recur.

**Fill** — • Label used to identify a brief melodic figure which is to be inserted into the arrangement.

**Rhy. Fill** — • A chordal version of a Fill.

**tacet** — • Instrument is silent (drops out).

• Repeat measures between signs.

• When a repeated section has different endings, play the first ending only the first time and the second ending only the second time.

**NOTE:** Tablature numbers in parentheses mean:
1. The note is being sustained over a system (note in standard notation is tied), or
2. The note is sustained, but a new articulation (such as a hammer-on, pull-off, slide or vibrato) begins, or
3. The note is a barely audible "ghost" note (note in standard notation is also in parentheses).

# HAL LEONARD GUITAR METHOD

## METHOD BOOKS, SONGBOOKS AND REFERENCE BOOKS

THE HAL LEONARD GUITAR METHOD is designed for anyone just learning to play acoustic or electric guitar. It is based on years of teaching guitar students of all ages, and it also reflects some of the best guitar teaching ideas from around the world. This comprehensive method includes: A learning sequence carefully paced with clear instructions; popular songs which increase the incentive to learn to play; versatility – can be used as self-instruction or with a teacher; audio accompaniments so that students have fun and sound great while practicing.

### BOOK 1
| | | |
|---|---|---|
| 00699010 | Book Only | $9.99 |
| 00699027 | Book/Online Audio | $14.99 |
| 00697341 | Book/Online Audio + DVD | $27.99 |
| 00697318 | DVD Only | $19.99 |
| 00155480 | Deluxe Beginner Edition (Book, CD, DVD, Online Audio/ Video & Chord Poster) | $22.99 |

### COMPLETE (BOOKS 1, 2 & 3)
| | | |
|---|---|---|
| 00699040 | Book Only | $19.99 |
| 00697342 | Book/Online Audio | $27.99 |

### BOOK 2
| | | |
|---|---|---|
| 00699020 | Book Only | $9.99 |
| 00697313 | Book/Online Audio | $14.99 |

### BOOK 3
| | | |
|---|---|---|
| 00699030 | Book Only | $9.99 |
| 00697316 | Book/Online Audio | $14.99 |

*Prices, contents and availability subject to change without notice.*

---

## STYLISTIC METHODS

### ACOUSTIC GUITAR
| | | |
|---|---|---|
| 00697347 | Method Book/Online Audio | $19.99 |
| 00237969 | Songbook/Online Audio | $17.99 |

### BLUEGRASS GUITAR
| | | |
|---|---|---|
| 00697405 | Method Book/Online Audio | $19.99 |

### BLUES GUITAR
| | | |
|---|---|---|
| 00697326 | Method Book/Online Audio (9" x 12") | $16.99 |
| 00697344 | Method Book/Online Audio (6" x 9") | $15.99 |
| 00697385 | Songbook/Online Audio (9" x 12") | $16.99 |
| 00248636 | Kids Method Book/Online Audio | $14.99 |

### BRAZILIAN GUITAR
| | | |
|---|---|---|
| 00697415 | Method Book/Online Audio | $17.99 |

### CHRISTIAN GUITAR
| | | |
|---|---|---|
| 00695947 | Method Book/Online Audio | $17.99 |

### CLASSICAL GUITAR
| | | |
|---|---|---|
| 00697376 | Method Book/Online Audio | $16.99 |

### COUNTRY GUITAR
| | | |
|---|---|---|
| 00697337 | Method Book/Online Audio | $24.99 |

### FINGERSTYLE GUITAR
| | | |
|---|---|---|
| 00697378 | Method Book/Online Audio | $22.99 |
| 00697432 | Songbook/Online Audio | $19.99 |

### FLAMENCO GUITAR
| | | |
|---|---|---|
| 00697363 | Method Book/Online Audio | $17.99 |

### FOLK GUITAR
| | | |
|---|---|---|
| 00697414 | Method Book/Online Audio | $16.99 |

### JAZZ GUITAR
| | | |
|---|---|---|
| 00695359 | Book/Online Audio | $22.99 |
| 00697386 | Songbook/Online Audio | $16.99 |

### JAZZ-ROCK FUSION
| | | |
|---|---|---|
| 00697387 | Book/Online Audio | $24.99 |

### R&B GUITAR
| | | |
|---|---|---|
| 00697356 | Book/Online Audio | $19.99 |
| 00697433 | Songbook/CD Pack | $16.99 |

### ROCK GUITAR
| | | |
|---|---|---|
| 00697319 | Book/Online Audio | $19.99 |
| 00697383 | Songbook/Online Audio | $19.99 |

### ROCKABILLY GUITAR
| | | |
|---|---|---|
| 00697407 | Book/Online Audio | $19.99 |

---

## OTHER METHOD BOOKS

### BARITONE GUITAR METHOD
| | | |
|---|---|---|
| 00242055 | Book/Online Audio | $12.99 |

### GUITAR FOR KIDS
| | | |
|---|---|---|
| 00865003 | Method Book 1/Online Audio | $14.99 |
| 00697402 | Songbook/Online Audio | $12.99 |
| 00128437 | Method Book 2/Online Audio | $14.99 |

### MUSIC THEORY FOR GUITARISTS
| | | |
|---|---|---|
| 00695790 | Book/Online Audio | $22.99 |

### TENOR GUITAR METHOD
| | | |
|---|---|---|
| 00148330 | Book/Online Audio | $14.99 |

### 12-STRING GUITAR METHOD
| | | |
|---|---|---|
| 00249528 | Book/Online Audio | $22.99 |

---

## METHOD SUPPLEMENTS

### ARPEGGIO FINDER
| | | |
|---|---|---|
| 00697352 | 6" x 9" Edition | $9.99 |
| 00697351 | 9" x 12" Edition | $10.99 |

### BARRE CHORDS
| | | |
|---|---|---|
| 00697406 | Book/Online Audio | $16.99 |

### CHORD, SCALE & ARPEGGIO FINDER
| | | |
|---|---|---|
| 00697410 | Book Only | $24.99 |

### GUITAR TECHNIQUES
| | | |
|---|---|---|
| 00697389 | Book/Online Audio | $16.99 |

### INCREDIBLE CHORD FINDER
| | | |
|---|---|---|
| 00697200 | 6" x 9" Edition | $7.99 |
| 00697208 | 9" x 12" Edition | $9.99 |

### INCREDIBLE SCALE FINDER
| | | |
|---|---|---|
| 00695568 | 6" x 9" Edition | $9.99 |
| 00695490 | 9" x 12" Edition | $9.99 |

### LEAD LICKS
| | | |
|---|---|---|
| 00697345 | Book/Online Audio | $12.99 |

### RHYTHM RIFFS
| | | |
|---|---|---|
| 00697346 | Book/Online Audio | $14.99 |

---

## SONGBOOKS

### CLASSICAL GUITAR PIECES
| | | |
|---|---|---|
| 00697388 | Book/Online Audio | $12.99 |

### EASY POP MELODIES
| | | |
|---|---|---|
| 00697281 | Book Only | $7.99 |
| 00697440 | Book/Online Audio | $16.99 |

### (MORE) EASY POP MELODIES
| | | |
|---|---|---|
| 00697280 | Book Only | $7.99 |
| 00697269 | Book/Online Audio | $16.99 |

### (EVEN MORE) EASY POP MELODIES
| | | |
|---|---|---|
| 00699154 | Book Only | $7.99 |
| 00697439 | Book/Online Audio | $16.99 |

### EASY POP RHYTHMS
| | | |
|---|---|---|
| 00697336 | Book Only | $10.99 |
| 00697441 | Book/Online Audio | $16.99 |

### (MORE) EASY POP RHYTHMS
| | | |
|---|---|---|
| 00697338 | Book Only | $9.99 |
| 00697322 | Book/Online Audio | $16.99 |

### (EVEN MORE) EASY POP RHYTHMS
| | | |
|---|---|---|
| 00697340 | Book Only | $9.99 |
| 00697323 | Book/Online Audio | $16.99 |

### EASY POP CHRISTMAS MELODIES
| | | |
|---|---|---|
| 00697417 | Book Only | $12.99 |
| 00697416 | Book/Online Audio | $16.99 |

### EASY POP CHRISTMAS RHYTHMS
| | | |
|---|---|---|
| 00278177 | Book Only | $6.99 |
| 00278175 | Book/Online Audio | $14.99 |

### EASY SOLO GUITAR PIECES
| | | |
|---|---|---|
| 00110407 | Book Only | $12.99 |

---

## REFERENCE

### GUITAR PRACTICE PLANNER
| | | |
|---|---|---|
| 00697401 | Book Only | $7.99 |

### GUITAR SETUP & MAINTENANCE
| | | |
|---|---|---|
| 00697427 | 6" x 9" Edition | $16.99 |
| 00697421 | 9" x 12" Edition | $14.99 |

For more info, songlists, or to purchase these and more books from your favorite music retailer, go to

**halleonard.com**

**HAL•LEONARD®**

# Get Better at Guitar

## ...with these Great Guitar Instruction Books from Hal Leonard!

### 101 GUITAR TIPS
**INCLUDES TAB**
Stuff All the Pros Know and Use

*by Adam St. James*
This book contains invaluable guidance on everything from scales and music theory to truss rod adjustments, proper recording studio set-ups, and much more.

00695737  Book/Online Audio ................................. $17.99

### AMAZING PHRASING
**INCLUDES TAB**
*by Tom Kolb*
This book/audio pack explores all the main components necessary for crafting well-balanced rhythmic and melodic phrases. It also explains how these phrases are put together to form cohesive solos. The companion audio contains 89 demo tracks, most with full-band backing.

00695583  Book/Online Audio ................................. $22.99

### ARPEGGIOS FOR THE MODERN GUITARIST
**INCLUDES TAB**
*by Tom Kolb*
Using this no-nonsense book with online audio, guitarists will learn to apply and execute all types of arpeggio forms using a variety of techniques, including alternate picking, sweep picking, tapping, string skipping, and legato.

00695862  Book/Online Audio ................................. $22.99

### BLUES YOU CAN USE

*by John Ganapes*
This comprehensive source for learning blues guitar is designed to develop both your lead and rhythm playing. Includes: 21 complete solos • blues chords, progressions and riffs • turnarounds • movable scales and soloing techniques • string bending • utilizing the entire fingerboard • and more.

00142420  Book/Online Media................................. $22.99

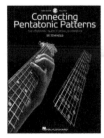

### CONNECTING PENTATONIC PATTERNS
**INCLUDES TAB**
*by Tom Kolb*
If you've been finding yourself trapped in the pentatonic box, this book is for you! This hands-on book with online audio offers examples for guitar players of all levels, from beginner to advanced. Study this book faithfully, and soon you'll be soloing all over the neck with the greatest of ease.

00696445  Book/Online Audio ................................. $24.99

### FRETBOARD MASTERY
**INCLUDES TAB**
*by Troy Stetina*
Untangle the mysterious regions of the guitar fretboard and unlock your potential. This book familiarizes you with all the shapes you need to know by applying them in real musical examples, thereby reinforcing and reaffirming your newfound knowledge.

00695331  Book/Online Audio ................................. $22.99

### GUITAR AEROBICS
**INCLUDES TAB**
*by Troy Nelson*
Here is a daily dose of guitar "vitamins" to keep your chops fine tuned! Musical styles include rock, blues, jazz, metal, country, and funk. Techniques taught include alternate picking, arpeggios, sweep picking, string skipping, legato, string bending, and rhythm guitar.

00695946  Book/Online Audio ................................. $24.99

### GUITAR CLUES
**INCLUDES TAB**
Operation Pentatonic

*by Greg Koch*
Whether you're new to improvising or have been doing it for a while, this book/audio pack will provide loads of delicious licks and tricks that you can use right away, from volume swells and chicken pickin' to intervallic and chordal ideas.

00695827  Book/Online Audio ................................. $24.99

### PAT METHENY – GUITAR ETUDES
**INCLUDES TAB**
Over the years, in many master classes and workshops around the world, Pat has demonstrated the kind of daily workout he puts himself through. This book includes a collection of 14 guitar etudes he created to help you limber up, improve picking technique and build finger independence.

00696587................................................................ $17.99

### PICTURE CHORD ENCYCLOPEDIA
This comprehensive guitar chord resource for all playing styles and levels features five voicings of 44 chord qualities for all twelve keys – 2,640 chords in all! For each, there is a clearly illustrated chord frame, as well as *an actual photo* of the chord being played!.

00695224................................................................ $22.99

### RHYTHM GUITAR 365
**INCLUDES TAB**
*by Troy Nelson*
This book provides 365 exercises – one for every day of the year! – to keep your rhythm chops fine tuned. Topics covered include: chord theory; the fundamentals of rhythm; fingerpicking; strum patterns; diatonic and non-diatonic progressions; triads; major and minor keys; and more.

00103627  Book/Online Audio ................................. $27.99

### SCALE CHORD RELATIONSHIPS
**INCLUDES TAB**
*by Michael Mueller & Jeff Schroedl*
This book/audio pack explains how to: recognize keys • analyze chord progressions • use the modes • play over nondiatonic harmony • use harmonic and melodic minor scales • use symmetrical scales • incorporate exotic scales • and much more!

00695563  Book/Online Audio ................................. $17.99

### SPEED MECHANICS FOR LEAD GUITAR
**INCLUDES TAB**
*by Troy Stetina*
Take your playing to the stratosphere with this advanced lead book which will help you develop speed and precision in today's explosive playing styles. Learn the fastest ways to achieve speed and control, secrets to make your practice time really count, and how to open your ears and make your musical ideas more solid and tangible.

00699323  Book/Online Audio ................................. $22.99

### TOTAL ROCK GUITAR
**INCLUDES TAB**
*by Troy Stetina*
This comprehensive source for learning rock guitar is designed to develop both lead and rhythm playing. It covers: getting a tone that rocks • open chords, power chords and barre chords • riffs, scales and licks • string bending, strumming, and harmonics • and more.

00695246  Book/Online Audio ................................. $22.99

*Guitar World Presents* **INCLUDES TAB**
### STEVE VAI'S GUITAR WORKOUT
In this book, Steve Vai reveals his path to virtuoso enlightenment with two challenging guitar workouts – one 10-hour and one 30-hour – which include scale and chord exercises, ear training, sight-reading, music theory, and much more.

00119643................................................................ $16.99

# HAL•LEONARD®